CVs and Applications

A beginner's guide

Jenny Barron, Tamsin Foxwell
and Debbie Steel

Student Helpbook Series

CVs and Applications – A beginner's guide

Seventh edition

Published by Lifetime Publishing, Mill House, Stallard Street, Trowbridge BA14 8HH

© Nord Anglia Lifetime Development South West Ltd, 2011

ISBN 978-1-904979-44-9

Printed by SS Media Ltd

Cover design by Arthouse Creative

Illustrations by Royston Robertson

Contents

About the authors

Jenny Barron, Tamsin Foxwell and Debbie Steel are part of the in-house author team at Lifetime Publishing. They contribute to the widely used CLIPS careers information system and have written a range of other student helpbooks and careers resources.

Acknowledgements

Thanks to Patricia McBride, author of the previous editions of *CVs and Applications*.

Introduction

If you're a young person and are thinking of applying for a job, an Apprenticeship or a course at college or university, then this book is for you! Perhaps you're feeling a bit unsure of the application process or you need to write your CV and don't know where to start. Whatever your situation, this book will guide you through the DOs and DON'Ts of CVs and applications.

If you've already looked for advice on writing your CV or completing an application form, you'll possibly feel swamped with information, much of which is contradictory or inappropriate. This book, however, is written especially for young people. With clear, practical advice and lots of helpful tips, *CVs and Applications* will equip you with the necessary tools and information you'll need to write a great CV or application form.

CVs and Applications is part of the Student Helpbook Series, which also includes *Excel at Interviews*, an ideal resource to help you prepare for your first interview.

Chapter one

Where to look for opportunities

"So where's the candy floss and the dodgems?"

The first stage of any application process is to find an opportunity you wish to apply for! This chapter will help you with that initial step by describing some of the best ways of searching for:

- jobs
- Apprenticeships
- college and university courses.

Finding such opportunities may be straightforward, or it may involve some creativity and perseverance on your part. This chapter describes the most typical places to look for opportunities, as well as some of the more informal approaches you could take.

Finding job vacancies

Employers may use a variety of methods to advertise their vacancies, and some people find job opportunities that have never been formally advertised at all! The internet is now, possibly, the most useful tool for any job search, but don't overlook the more traditional approaches, such as checking newspaper adverts or visiting your local Connexions/ careers service, as these still deliver results and may be the best option for finding certain types of jobs. When looking for work, it makes sense to try as many different approaches listed here as possible, in order to find the full range of opportunities available at any one time.

Connexions, Careers Wales and Jobcentre Plus

Connexions, Careers Wales and Jobcentre Plus are public services that can help you find work. They hold information about local employers and the local labour market, and their staff are trained to provide you with advice and support while you are job hunting. In particular, they keep details of current vacancies in your area and can help you apply for any that interest you. The service that is most appropriate for you will depend on where you live and your age.

In England, if you are aged up to 19 (or 25 if you have a learning difficulty or disability) you can get help and advice with your job search through your local Connexions service. These services have good contacts with local employers and keep details of current vacancies that are suitable for young people. Many Connexions services also post details of local vacancies on their websites. To find details of your local service, visit www.connexions-direct.com.

If you are aged 16 to 19 and live in Wales, you can search for vacancies through the Careers Wales service. This service runs Careers Shops and Careers Centres, which you can visit in order to view details of local vacancies on their job boards. Alternatively, you can search online for vacancies in Wales at www.careerswales.com.

Anyone of working age can use the services of their local Jobcentre Plus (although you may be redirected to your local Connexions/Careers Wales service if you are under 18). You can search for jobs by visiting your local Jobcentre Plus office and using one of the touch-screen Jobpoints.

Alternatively, you can:

- phone the Jobcentre Plus job-matching service, on 0845 6060 234 (textphone: 0845 6055 255)

- search for Jobcentre Plus vacancies online by selecting the 'Employment' section of the Directgov website: www.direct.gov.uk

- view Jobcentre Plus vacancies through the Directgov service on digital TV (Sky and Virgin Media)

- access a job search facility through your mobile phone (as long as it is internet enabled) by typing m.direct.gov.uk/jobs into your phone's internet browser

- use the free Jobcentre Plus job search 'app', if you have an iPhone, iPod touch or Google Android phone.

Employers' websites

If you know which organisations offer the type of work you are interested in, have a look at their websites to see if they list their vacancies online. In particular, many medium to large organisations have sections of their websites dedicated to careers information that may, in addition to advertising their current vacancies, tell you more about what it would be like to work for them.

Even if the employer doesn't have any vacancies of interest to you when you first look, it is often possible to sign up to an 'alert' service that will send you an email automatically, as soon as the employer advertises a new position. If you are familiar with RSS feeds, you may also find that some employers use these to highlight any new vacancies that they have posted.

A fairly recent trend is for employers to use social networking websites to post details of their vacancies. For example, some organisations have signed up to *Facebook* or *Twitter* – if you sign up also, you can become a 'fan' or 'follow' any of these organisations and receive a notification when they post a new vacancy. Take care that your own online profile does not contain anything that may put off a potential employer, as they may take the opportunity to check your details too!

Online job sites

There are a huge number of websites that list vacancies on behalf of employers. These vary from general sites that advertise all types of jobs to sites that specialise in a particular employment sector.

Online job sites are often very sophisticated, allowing you to:

- search for jobs that meet your particular preferences
- save details of your search criteria, so that you can quickly perform the same search time and time again
- create a CV using an online template
- upload your CV so that potential employers can search for you
- apply for vacancies quickly and easily using a standard CV and covering letter
- keep track of your applications
- sign up for an 'alert' service, so that you receive an email telling you when new jobs have been posted that meet your criteria.

Some of the most popular, general job sites include:

www.direct.gov.uk/jobsearch (an online service operated by the Jobcentre Plus)
www.monster.co.uk
www.totaljobs.com
www.reed.co.uk
www.redgoldfish.co.uk
www.jobsite.co.uk.

Some employers may favour specialist job sites, rather than general ones, because they allow them to target their adverts at exactly the right type of applicants. For an easy way to see if there are any online job sites that specialise in the type of work that interests you, simply use a search engine, such as *Google*, to search for a term along the lines of 'engineering jobs', 'retail jobs' or whatever is appropriate for you.

In many cases, professional bodies and trade associations also advertise specialist vacancies on their websites, so it is worth looking out for any such organisations that are relevant to the type of work that interests you.

Newspapers and journals

Most national and local newspapers, as well as a great many journals, are now available both in a paper format and online. While fewer employers are placing vacancy adverts in paper versions of newspapers and journals these days, you may still find some jobs advertised this way. It is much more common for employers to place job adverts with the online versions.

Local newspapers, and their associated websites, are most likely to feature jobs that are suitable for people straight out of school or college, as well as a range of other vacancies. The paper versions of local newspapers only carry adverts for jobs that are based in the local area. However, their equivalent online versions often allow you to search for jobs nationwide.

The national newspaper brands tend to advertise specialist jobs requiring a high level of qualifications or experience, such as those targeting graduates or professionals with several years of experience. Certain national newspaper brands (i.e. both the online and paper formats) are well known for advertising certain types of jobs. For example:

- *Guardian* – popular for public sector, marketing, media and charity vacancies

- *The Telegraph* – good for IT, accountancy, and science and technology vacancies

- *The Times* – well known for business and finance, education and research, and legal vacancies.

There are many different professional journals, as well as those concerned with general interests, such as *New Scientist*, that carry job adverts relating to their subject matter. If you are uncertain whether there is a journal relevant to the type of work that interests you, try asking your personal/careers adviser, visiting your local library or searching online. Just a few examples include *VNJ* (Veterinary Nursing Journal), *Legal Executive Journal*, *Caterer and Hotelkeeper*, and *HSJ* (Health Service Journal). While you could subscribe to any journals that interest you, this may prove to be an expensive option; instead, you could see if you local library stocks copies or check to see whether there is an online version.

Employment agencies

Employment agencies (also known as recruitment agencies) can be found in most towns and cities. Employers use agencies to help them find suitable candidates when they have a vacancy. Agencies advertise jobs in exactly the same ways as an employer might (through online job sites, in newspapers, on their own websites and so on). The difference is that, as an applicant, you first apply to the agency, which will assess your suitability for the position before deciding whether or not to put you forward to the employer. Even if an agency is not currently advertising any roles that are of interest to you, you can still register with them so that they can keep your details on file and let you know when any suitable jobs arise.

Agencies vary in size and scope. There are some large employment agencies (such as Reed, Randstad and Manpower) with branches nationwide; others are small, independent firms that just cover a single town. Some agencies specialise in particular types of work, such as construction or media jobs. Many agencies advertise both permanent and temporary positions. There is nothing to stop you registering with several agencies in order to increase you chances of being put forward for as many vacancies as possible.

It is important to remember that agencies are working on behalf of the employer – not you! You will need to make a good impression on the agency staff in order for them to feel happy to put you forward for any jobs. The agency may conduct preliminary assessments on behalf of the employer – for example, testing your wordprocessing skills or numeracy (Chapter ten has more information about these, and other, types of tests). You will also need to take responsibility for keeping in touch with any agencies that you have registered with, letting them know of any changes to your circumstances and your continued interest in finding work through them.

Note that agencies are not allowed to charge you for registering with them.

Applying 'on spec'

It is always possible for you to contact an employer speculatively (or on spec) to find out whether they have any suitable opportunities. To be as effective as possible, this approach requires you to do some research so that you can really target your efforts. Find out:

- which organisations offer the type of work that interests you

- what their current situation is like – a growing business is likely to have more opportunities in the near future than one that has recently cut back its operations

- who is responsible for recruiting staff – find out their name, job title and contact details.

You could try writing to the recruiting manager, either by sending a letter or email, and attaching your CV. Use your covering letter/email to explain why you particularly want to work for that organisation, summarising what you have to offer and asking for your details to be kept on file and considered for any future vacancies that arise (for more information on covering letters, see Chapter nine). Make sure your contact details are clearly stated so that it is easy for the recruiting manager to get back in touch with you if they want to find out more about you. If you have not heard back within a week or so, be prepared to make a follow-up phone call to make sure your letter has reached the most appropriate person and to find out whether you would be considered for any upcoming vacancies.

Alternatively, you could try phoning the recruiting manager to talk through what opportunities may be available now or in the future. Think very carefully about how you would approach such a conversation. Remember you will be taking up the time of a manager who may be very busy or who may not foresee any vacancies arising in the near future. If, however, they are happy to chat to you, try to find out more about what type of work their organisation undertakes, what type of skills and qualifications they look for, and whether there are any opportunities coming up. Briefly describe what you could offer the organisation (in terms of skills, qualifications etc) and explain why you are particularly interested in working for them. Remain polite and professional at all times, and thank them for taking the time to speak to you, even if the conversation does not result in any useful outcomes.

Note that some organisations do not accept on spec applications, while others may only hold your details on file for a limited period of time. It is therefore a good idea to find out in advance what approach the employer takes, so that you know how effective applying on spec might be for you.

School and college careers departments

If you are still in education, make sure you find out whether your school or college keeps details of any local opportunities by speaking to your careers coordinator or another member of staff involved with the careers department. Your school or college may be notified of work and training opportunities by your local Connexions/careers service, or directly by employers and training organisations. If so, vacancies may be displayed on a notice board or through your school's or college's internal website.

Networking

Networking is all about building relationships with people who may be able to help you find work. You could consider all of your friends and family as a starting point. For example, if one of your friends works for a company that you like the sound of, ask them whether it has any opportunities that might suit you and whether they could put your name forward for them. It is especially helpful if they could also personally recommend you to the recruiting manager, as long as they are happy to do so!

To extend your network, you will need to take the opportunity to promote yourself to people that you meet in a variety of situations – at parties or sporting events, careers fairs or through work experience etc. Networking does not involve asking people for a job outright – that would make for a very uncomfortable conversation! Instead, take the time to find out about where the other person works and what they do. Mention that you are looking for a job and ask if they have any tips for getting into that line of work. They may be able to refer you on to someone who is responsible for recruiting in their company, if appropriate, or give you some other advice that will help your job search.

Networking can become an increasingly effective way of finding out about opportunities and promoting yourself, the older you get. In every job that you do, you will work with colleagues and external suppliers or customers involved in the same business or industry as you. By building good relationships with as many of these people as possible, you will create a network of people that you can turn to, should you ever find yourself out of work or looking to move jobs.

The internet offers a variety of opportunities for networking. Many websites, such as *Facebook* and *MySpace*, for example, involve developing a network of friends or contacts. The website *LinkedIn* (www.linkedin.com), in particular, is popular with people who want to build a network of professional contacts. If you are going to use such websites as part of your job search, make sure that your online profile has nothing that could put off a potential employer, such as rude comments, embarrassing photos or anything that makes you appear unprofessional!

Careers fairs

Careers fairs are often run by Connexions/careers services, schools, colleges and universities, as well as by some commercial organisations. Careers fairs give you the opportunity to meet with a wide range of employers who are looking to recruit significant numbers of new employees. The most common careers fairs are those relating to graduate recruitment, often run by universities and aimed at undergraduates in their final year of studies. Some careers fairs may be targeted at people wanting to work in a particular sector, such as careers using languages or careers in engineering and construction.

If you are still in education, you will probably be made aware of any upcoming careers fairs in your area by your careers coordinator or personal/careers adviser. Look out for posters, emails or online adverts (on your school, college or university website) for details of relevant events. If you are particularly interested in graduate careers fairs, the *Prospects* website (www.prospects.ac.uk) lists nationwide events. Once you have left education, you may see careers fairs advertised in local papers or try using *Google*, for example, to search for events online.

In order to get the most out of a careers fair, it makes sense to do some preparation and research beforehand.

- Check which employers will be attending the event and find out what they do and the type of work opportunities they offer. When you attend the event, you can then target the ones that are of most interest to you – and speak knowledgeably about how you could fit into their organisation.

- Make a note of any questions you would like to ask, perhaps about training, career progression, the application process and so on.

- Think about what to wear and how to present yourself. Most employers will appreciate you dressing in smart clothes and be prepared to talk about your skills, qualifications, interests and career aspirations.

- Print and take several copies of your CV – you can hand it in to any employers that are of interest to you.

It is unlikely that you will be offered a job right there and then, however, do treat careers fairs as an important stage in the recruitment process. It is possible that the people you meet on the stands will have some say in deciding who may get invited for a more formal interview at a later date, or who ultimately is offered a job.

Of course, careers fairs also give you the chance to find out more about employers and what it might be like to work for them, so take full advantage of talking to as many people as possible to find out more about what opportunities are on offer. There may be brochures or other handouts that you can take away; if not, make sure you make a note of any contact details that will come in useful later on.

Getting your 'foot in the door'

It is surprising how many people are offered a permanent job after they have worked for an organisation in some other capacity. If you have an opportunity to undertake a work experience placement or an internship, or if you have a part-time or 'temp' job, you will be in a very good position to apply for any jobs that arise with that organisation.

It is not unheard of for organisations to offer such workers a permanent position without formally advertising a vacancy. However, most organisations follow a formal recruitment process that requires you to apply for the job in competition with others. Even so, you will have an advantage over any external candidates, as you will have gained useful insight about the role on offer, relevant experience about how the organisation operates, and, hopefully, a good reputation about your skills and attitude.

In particular, it is becoming increasingly common for large, prestigious companies to use internships as a means of assessing candidates before accepting them onto their graduate training schemes.

Setting up your own website

There are certain occasions when setting up your own website can be useful, but it is by no means essential. For example, if you want a job in art and design, a website can be used to easily store and display your portfolio of work. Alternatively, if you want to work in computer programming, software design, website design or a related field, setting up your own website is a very good way of demonstrating that you have relevant skills to a potential employer.

If you choose to go down this route, make sure that everything about your website works as intended, any text is spelled correctly, and that you keep the content professional. Remember that, in most situations, an employer is unlikely to find your website by chance; you will have to promote it by including the web address on your CV etc.

Shop windows and notice boards

There are just a few types of jobs that you may find advertised in shop windows or company notice boards. For example, a hairdressing salon may put a notice in its window that it is looking for a new stylist, a large hospital may have a notice board with a list of current vacancies, and so on. Keep your eyes peeled when you are out and about and ask friends and family to tell you about any jobs that they see advertised where they work.

Finding Apprenticeships

Apprenticeships offer structured training with an employer and combine work with part-time study at a college or with a training provider. As such, you may be able to find Apprenticeship opportunities advertised by employers as well as by colleges and training organisations. The other sections in this chapter describe how to find job vacancies and college courses, some of which may include Apprenticeship opportunities, so you can use these approaches to search for Apprenticeships also.

You can also search for Apprenticeship opportunities online using the Apprenticeship Matching Service. For opportunities in England, this is available through the National Apprenticeship Service's website at www.apprenticeships.org.uk, while in Wales the matching service can be accessed via the Careers Wales website at www.careerswales.com.

Alternatively, contact your local Connexions/careers service for details of Apprenticeships, or other jobs with training, in your area.

Finding college and university courses

There are a variety of ways for you to find out which courses are available – and where, and these are listed below. However, if you need any help or advice, staff at your local Connexions/careers service will be able to assist you or ask a teacher or careers coordinator at your school or college.

Make sure that, whichever source of information you use, the information is up to date, as vital information, such as entry requirements or financial arrangements, can change from one year to the next.

If you know which college or university you wish to attend...

All colleges and universities produce a prospectus, which lists details of all the courses they have on offer. If you want to have a look at a paper version of the prospectuses for colleges and universities in your local area, you should be able to obtain copies from a number of sources:

- your school careers department
- your local Connexions/careers centre
- your local library

- the college or university itself – request a copy by phone or online, or simply drop in to pick up a copy in person.

Alternatively, most colleges and universities also publish their prospectuses online via their websites. These may be available simply to view on-screen or print out, while some college and university websites make it easy for you to browse and search for courses online.

If you know which course you want to take...

There are a number of websites that offer course search facilities if you are not sure which college or university offers the course you are looking for.

In England, a fairly recent development is the online **14–19 Prospectus** (sometimes known as the **Area-Wide Prospectus**). This allows you to search through all the courses, qualifications and training opportunities available for 14- to 19-year-olds in your region. Courses include those offered by further education colleges, sixth form colleges, schools and so on. Each region has its own website; to find the website covering your area, visit www.direct.gov.uk/14-19prospectus.

In Wales, you can search for courses and training opportunities via the Careers Wales website at www.careerswales.com. This offers options for narrowing your search according to age group and region.

The Next Step service is aimed at adults and offers a course search facility. You can either call the service on 0800 100 900 or visit the website at www.direct.gov.uk/nextstep.

For full-time higher education courses (including degrees, HNDs and foundation degrees), the most comprehensive source of information is available through UCAS, which is the organisation that manages applications to UK higher education courses. UCAS provides the following resources you can use to search for courses:

- the *Big Guide* – a course directory that may be available in school, college or Connexions/careers service libraries; an accompanying CD-ROM provides a quick and easy way to check entry requirements for any courses of interest to you

- an online course search facility at www.ucas.com.

To find details of both full- and part-time foundation degree courses, visit the Foundation Degree Forward website at www.fdf.ac.uk.

If you need inspiration...

Perhaps you are thinking about going on to further or higher education but are not sure which course would suit you or where you might study. Your teacher or careers coordinator will be able to help you understand your options in the first instance, or ask to see your personal/careers adviser for guidance. Careers fairs (as described earlier) often have representatives from local colleges, universities or training providers that you can speak to, so may also be worth attending as a source of ideas. If you are particularly interested in higher education courses, UCAS stages various conventions and subject-specific exhibitions (covering art and design, media and performing arts, for example) – visit www.ucas.com for more information.

Chapter two

Understanding the
selection process

This chapter will help you:

- identify what selectors are looking for

- appreciate the importance of targeting your applications

- understand how selectors create a shortlist of applicants.

However skilled or talented you may be, you will only be successful when applying for a job or course if you can offer what the selector is looking for. Selectors, in the case of job and Apprenticeship applications, may include the team leader or manager of the role in question, senior managers and members of the human resources (HR) department. If you are applying for a course, an admissions tutor is usually responsible for selecting which candidates will be taken on as students.

The selection process for job vacancies

Most organisations have a standard recruitment procedure that is followed whenever a vacancy arises. It typically involves:

- creating an up-to-date **job description** – a document that lists all the tasks and responsibilities that the job-holder would be expected to undertake

- writing a **person specification** (also known as a 'person spec') – a list of the essential and desirable qualifications, experience and other qualities that a person needs in order to do the job

- listing the **competencies** required for the job – the skills, knowledge and behaviours an employee will be displaying when performing tasks correctly (Chapter four has more information on competencies)

- producing an **advert**, which summarises the main points of the job description, person spec and competencies, as well as giving some background information about the job and organisation, the benefits of working there, and instructions on how to apply.

These pieces of information will be crucial to your application, so make sure you take time to read and consider them all carefully.

Starting with the advert – there should be enough information here to give you some idea of whether you are interested in the role and whether you would make a suitable candidate. Make sure you keep a copy of any adverts you decide to respond to, as there can be useful descriptive information here (about the organisation and its culture, for example) that you may not be able to find elsewhere. An advert should also indicate how you can obtain copies of the relevant person spec, job description and competencies, if applicable.

Once you've got hold of a copy of the job description, it is important that you consider this information carefully. Some job descriptions use very formal language that can be quite hard to understand. For example, 'liaise with external suppliers to ensure deliveries meet agreed timeframes' may simply mean 'phone our suppliers to check they are going to deliver our orders on time'! If you are in any doubt about what the job involves, contact the employer for further information – they will be happy to talk to you about the vacancy.

Next, the person spec – this is where the employer will have set out in very clear terms what they are looking for. Employers have to be able to show that they have treated all applicants fairly, and haven't discriminated, for example, on the grounds of race or religion. A person spec allows employers to measure each applicant against the same criteria, and reject those that don't meet their requirements. Some criteria will be **essential** – if you do not meet these, you will be automatically rejected. Some criteria will be **desirable** – if you can demonstrate that you can meet any of these criteria it will help your application, but the final decision may rest on other factors.

A vacancy for a trainee customer services adviser, for example, might have a person spec as follows:

	Essential	**Desirable**
Qualifications	5 GCSEs including English and maths at grades A*-C (or equivalent)	2 A levels (or equivalent)
Experience	Experience of answering customer queries Experience of working in the retail sector	Experience of responding to customer complaints Experience of leading a team
Knowledge		Knowledge of the company's product range
Skills	Excellent customer service skills Excellent communication skills MS Word	Presentation skills MS Excel
Personal attributes	Organised Good at problem solving Able to meet deadlines Enthusiastic	

Finally, the list of competencies – not all employers set out the competencies required, but where they do exist, they typically set out what types of skills, knowledge and behaviour are appropriate for each level of job. For example, if dealing with customer complaints is part of the job description:

- for an assistant, this may mean accurately recording the customer's complaint and passing it on to an appropriate member of staff to deal with

- for a manager, this may mean investigating the complaint, responding to the customer and resolving the problem to the customer's satisfaction.

By examining the advert, job description, person spec and competencies, you should be able to form a very good idea of what the employer is looking for. You can now use this information to tailor your application to clearly demonstrate that you meet most, if not all, of the employer's requirements.

Note, however, that not all employers will follow this approach; some smaller employers, in particular, may be much more informal. They may provide much less information about the opportunity on offer, or it may be presented in a more basic way. If, for whatever reason, you don't feel that the employer has supplied enough information about what the job involves or what type of person they are looking for, remember you can always contact them to find out more.

Targeting your job application

The benefits of targeting your application

It may be tempting to create one CV and one covering letter and send copies of them to each and every job you want to apply for. In a similar way, it can seem easier to write standard responses in every application form you complete. While this approach will certainly save you time, it may not be very effective! Try to think of it from the employer's point of view:

- they may have lots of applicants to consider, so want to quickly and easily identify those that meet the essential and desirable criteria from the job spec

- they want to find an enthusiastic and committed employee, so will be looking for evidence of your interest in their particular vacancy, rather than any job in general

- if you don't put any effort into tailoring your application to their specific vacancy, they may wonder how much effort you will put into your work!

So, it really makes a lot of sense to target your application to the specific requirements of each particular vacancy.

How to target your application

In order to target your application, you first need to understand what the selector is looking for. Use the job advert, job description, person spec and list of competencies to work out what qualifications, skills and experience the selector considers **relevant** and rank them in order of **importance**.

- The list of essential criteria, as given on the person spec, is your starting point. The main purpose of your CV or application form is to provide evidence of how you meet each of these criteria – so this is the most important information you need to get across.

- If you can demonstrate how you meet any of the desirable criteria then that is the next thing to concentrate on.

- Check the job advert, list of competencies and any other sources of information you may have about the job and organisation (from their website, recruitment brochures, news reports etc) to see if there are any other ways you can match your skills and knowledge to their requirements.

Whether you are required to complete an application form or submit your CV, the type of information selectors ask for is broadly the same. They need factual information about your contact details, dates in education, qualifications gained, work experience and so on. These facts about your life can't be changed. However, how you **present** these facts can be changed and adapted for each application.

What targeting your application can mean:

- emphasising the most relevant information about yourself – for example, by changing the order of items, so that the most important information comes first, or by formatting key points in bold

- describing how your work experience or other achievements enabled you to develop skills and knowledge that are relevant to this job, rather than just listing the tasks involved

- only including information that is relevant to the job you are applying for

- thinking hard about what evidence you can give that best shows you meet the criteria (Chapters three and four have advice about this)

- providing information in the same order as the list of essential/ desirable criteria (if possible), as this will help the selector quickly identify and tick off which criteria you meet

- including a covering letter summarising why you want to work for this particular organisation in this particular role, and briefly describing the most relevant qualifications, skills and experience you have to offer (see Chapter nine for more information about covering letters).

What targeting your application **does not** mean:

- lying about your achievements or experiences

- withholding information that the selector has specifically requested, even if you are worried it will show you in a bad light. Remember, you can always use your covering letter to explain any particular problems you have had in the past.

How do employers shortlist?

A job advert may result in any number of people applying – from a handful to a hundred or more! However many applications are received, the employer has to decide which candidates to invite for an interview. In most cases there will be too many applicants to interview them all, so the employer must select the top few candidates (often, just the top four or five will be invited). The employer may use a variety of criteria to sift through the applications, in order to create the 'shortlist' for interview.

In the first instance, employers may reject those applications that make a poor first impression. For example, you may automatically be rejected if your application is:

- received after the deadline – if you can't get your application in by the date requested, employers will wonder whether you take the same approach with your work

- incomplete and missing information specifically requested by the employer – employers will have asked for that information for a reason and may assume the worst if you don't supply it, plus they will want to see that you can follow instructions

- full of errors (such as spelling mistakes or factual mistakes about the job you are applying for) – most jobs require attention to detail and a careful approach to your work, so you need to demonstrate these qualities in your application also

- poorly presented – you need to impress an employer and show that you take care with your work; in particular, if you make it hard for a selector to find the information they are looking for in your application, they may not bother to go hunting for it!

Any applications that remain as possibilities after this first sift will then be more closely examined. This is when the employer will refer to the person spec, described earlier, and start judging each applicant against the **essential criteria** set out in that document. The employer will look at your CV or application form, as well as any covering letter that you have supplied, and check for evidence that you have all of the essential skills, qualifications, experience and so on. Any applications that meet the essential criteria will be kept, and the rest rejected.

Remaining applications may then be assessed against the **desirable criteria**, as listed on the person spec. Some of these criteria may be judged to be more important than others, so that will be taken into consideration also.

By now, the employer will have reduced the number of potential candidates, but if there are still too many to interview, they will have to start making decisions based on other factors. They may consider the following:

- do some candidates have more relevant experience, skills or qualifications than the others?

- have some candidates demonstrated higher levels of competency than the others?

- do some candidates come across as more enthusiastic and passionate about the job in their covering letter than the others?

- are some candidates available to start the job sooner than the others?

- do some candidates have lower salary expectations than the others?

As you can see, you might be unsuccessful in your application for reasons that are beyond your control. You are unlikely to ever know the other candidates you are up against, so it is not worth worrying about the competition; the only thing you can control is how well you present yourself through your application.

On some occasions, none of the applicants will meet all of the essential criteria. While the employer may choose to re-advertise the role, they may instead decide to lower their criteria. So it can still be worth applying for a job, even if you cannot offer exactly what the employer is looking for – they may just consider you to be the best applicant and hire you anyway!

The selection process for Apprenticeships

The selection process for an Apprenticeship is like that of any other job. A recruiting manager shortlists candidates to interview based on them meeting the requirements of the role, as set out in a person spec, etc. In addition, however, the recruiting manager will also need to assess whether candidates have the motivation and ability to complete the necessary training, which typically involves part-time attendance at a college or training centre and may involve assignments, workplace assessments or exams. The selection process may well include aptitude tests (to check your numeracy and literacy, for example) – Chapter ten has more information on what these tests might involve.

Targeting you Apprenticeship application

It is important that when applying for an Apprenticeship you think about how to show you have the skills and abilities to do the job, as well as the commitment and interest to complete all aspects of the training. You may be able to use examples from your life of when you have had to be self-motivated in order to see a project through to the end, or when you have had to deliver several pieces of coursework to a tight deadline, for instance. There are more tips about applying for Apprenticeships in Chapter eight.

The selection process for college and university courses

Colleges and universities run many courses each year; each course has certain entry requirements that are set out in prospectuses and online course descriptions. In the case of full-time higher education (HE) courses, entry requirements are also available through UCAS either online at www.ucas.com or in the *Big Guide* and its accompanying CD-ROM, which is available through most school, college and Connexions/career service libraries.

Course entry requirements usually focus on your academic ability and may state that you need:

- a certain number of qualifications, e.g. four GCSEs

- qualifications at a particular level, e.g. level 3 qualifications (A levels, Advanced Diplomas, BTEC Level 3 Nationals etc)

- qualifications in particular subjects

- specific grades, or a certain number of UCAS Tariff points in the case of HE courses.

Certain courses may set other entry requirements, such as relevant work experience or completion of specific admission tests (which are described in more detail in Chapter ten).

What is the selection process?

Admissions staff, who are usually course tutors related to your chosen subject, are responsible for deciding which applicants to accept.

In the case of colleges of further education (FE) and sixth form colleges, the emphasis is on matching applicants to the most suitable course for them. After you have applied for a course, it is likely that you will be invited for an informal chat or interview with a tutor to make sure you are selecting the best course for you, based on your ability, interests and future career intentions. You can usually apply for courses throughout the year before the course start date, but apply as early as possible for popular courses, to avoid missing out on a place.

The selection process for HE courses, such as degrees and HNDs, focuses mainly on your academic potential, although other factors may be taken into consideration. For example, if you intend to apply for degree courses in subjects such as social work, medicine or dental surgery, you will need to show evidence of your commitment and motivation to these types of work, through relevant work experience or voluntary activities. Whereas, for art and design courses, you will have to present a portfolio of your work to support your application.

Targeting your course application

Unlike applications for job vacancies, you may find that you only have the opportunity to submit one application in relation to several possible courses. For example, the UCAS application process involves writing one 'personal statement' in support of up to five different courses. Likewise, in many areas, a Common Application Process is being introduced that enables students to apply online for any post-16 opportunity, using potentially just a single application. Targeting your application to each individual course that interests you, therefore, maybe somewhat hard to do.

Where possible, though, it is still worth making clear in your application why this particular course at this particular institution is of interest to you, what relevant skills and experience you have, and how this course relates to your future career goals. For courses where there are more applicants than places, admissions tutors will look for evidence that you have a good understanding of what the course is about and are motivated to complete it. Chapter eight provides further advice about applying for courses.

Chapter three

Understanding yourself

"Where do you see yourself in five years? Please do not say 'In your chair'..."

This chapter will help you:

- think about who you are and what you want

- assess what you have to offer

- present any negative information in a positive light.

Recruiting managers and admissions tutors usually gain their first impression of you from your CV or application form. Knowing how to present yourself effectively to them not only involves understanding what they are looking for, but understanding yourself too.

What's important to you?

Whether you are applying for a job or a course, most selectors will want to find out something about your reasons for applying – what motivates you, how committed you are, your career goals and so on. It is this type of information that may be the deciding factor between two candidates who have very similar qualifications and experience. Selectors will be looking for someone who is motivated and enthusiastic about the opportunity on offer.

Whenever you apply for a job or course, identify your **positive** reasons for wanting to apply for this **particular** opportunity and try to include these in your application. It will show that you have considered carefully the opportunity on offer and that it suits you, and you suit it!

Most application forms will give you the opportunity to outline briefly your reasons for applying, while if you are submitting a CV, it may be useful to include some of your reasons in your covering letter.

For example, if you are applying for a job, consider the following.

- **Why do you want to work for this organisation?** Think about what's special about this organisation and why it matters to you. For example, is it a growing business, a leader in its sector, a small and flexible company, an organisation that has certain ethics and values, or does it operate in a sector you feel particularly passionate about (such as sport, fashion, animal welfare etc)?

- **What appeals to you about this vacancy?** Consider how this job would make good use of your skills and aptitudes. For instance, if you are outgoing, creative, analytical or caring, does this job let you make the most of these qualities? Does the role involve things you enjoy doing, such as working with your hands, being outdoors, dealing with people or organising events?

- **How does it fit with your long-term career goals?** Are you committed to working in this sector, undertaking relevant training and progressing in this type of work? Does the organisation offer ongoing training, the chance for rapid promotion, or opportunities to progress your career in a variety of directions?

If you are applying for a course, consider the following.

- **How is the course taught and assessed?** Think about your preferred style of learning. Do you enjoy practical lessons, lectures, group work or essay writing, for example? Are you more comfortable being assessed through exams, coursework or practical assignments?

- **What interests you about the subject?** Does the course cover particular topics that are of interest to you, is it a broad-based course or will you develop in-depth knowledge of a specialist topic?

- **How does it fit with your long-term career goals?** Think about how this course will help you progress. Is it essential for your chosen career, will it give you an advantage when you come to apply for jobs, or does it help keep your options open while you still decide on a career path?

Assessing what you have to offer

The main purpose of a CV or application form is to 'sell' yourself based on the relevant skills and experience you have to offer. You will develop all sorts of knowledge and expertise during the course of your life, and even when you are just starting out, you still have plenty to offer.

Transferable skills

When trying to assess your skills, remember to consider all aspects of your life. Many skills are 'transferable', meaning that skills gained in one situation can be used in (or transferred to) a different situation. A good starting point may be to think about the experiences you have gained in any of the following situations.

- **School or college** – did your studies involve project work, internet research, presentations to the class, essay writing, meeting deadlines, working in teams, etc? Did you hold any positions of responsibility?

- **Paid work** (full or part time) – what were your responsibilities, did you receive any training, who did you deal with, did you use any special tools or equipment, etc?

- **Volunteering** – have you contributed as a volunteer to any particular project or cause, what did you do, who did you deal with, did it require any training, etc?

- **Work experience** – what tasks were you involved in, did you receive any training, were you given responsibility for any particular work, etc?

- **Your home life** – do you cook, clean or do any gardening; do you look after any younger brothers or sisters; do you help manage the family budget; do you use a language other than English at home; do you care for any sick or elderly relatives, etc?

- **Your hobbies and interests** – are you involved in any clubs or societies, do you contribute to how they are run, have you organised any events, do your hobbies or interests involve any particular skills, do you receive any coaching or training, do you coach or train others, how much time and commitment is involved, etc?

- **Other life experiences** – have you had to deal with any difficult experiences (such as major illness or a disrupted home life); have you learned to drive; are you fluent in any other languages; do you spend a lot of time using computers; have you done any travelling, etc?

You should be able to identify certain skills that these experiences have helped you to develop. The following lists provide a few suggestions for you.

Communication skills

- expressing yourself clearly
- presenting to a group
- teaching others
- writing reports
- debating
- explaining complicated ideas
- summarising
- listening well
- asking questions
- negotiating
- translating or knowledge of another language
- liaising
- advising
- selling

People skills

- motivating others
- leading a team
- supporting others
- caring for others
- teamworking
- mentoring
- counselling
- giving feedback
- helping
- customer service
- finding a compromise
- resolving conflict
- entertaining

Practical skills

- fixing things
- making things
- keyboarding
- filing
- driving
- first aid
- playing a musical instrument
- cooking
- carpentry
- metalwork
- gardening
- sewing

Scientific and technical skills

- designing websites
- computer programming
- conducting experiments
- observing
- recording and editing (audio and video)
- recording data
- using maps

Organisational skills

- planning
- arranging
- time management
- prioritising
- monitoring
- scheduling
- decision making

Numeracy skills

- budgeting
- calculating
- analysing
- estimating
- producing graphs
- forecasting

Creative skills

- drawing
- designing
- photography
- composing music

- creative writing
- painting
- dancing
- acting
- image editing

Thinking skills

- drawing conclusions
- checking
- making recommendations
- generating ideas
- researching
- sorting
- questioning
- inspecting
- devising
- solving problems

Specific skills

You may be able to think of many other valuable skills that you have to offer. Some may not be transferable, but should obviously be mentioned if they are relevant to the particular opportunity on offer. For example, you may have skills relating to a specific:

- occupation (such as hairdressing, bricklaying or farming)
- computer software package
- piece of equipment.

Remember that, if you are just starting out and applying for a job or course, selectors are unlikely to expect such specific skills. Instead, they will be looking for your potential to develop them, as well as your enthusiasm to gain them.

Your personality

It may help the selector to get a better sense of how you would fit into the organisation or onto a course if you can include a brief description of your personality. Think about the positive ways you can describe yourself. Some examples include:

- enthusiastic
- cheerful
- energetic
- proactive
- friendly
- mature outlook
- keen to learn
- reliable
- careful
- flexible
- self-motivated
- conscientious
- responsible
- hard working
- ambitious.

It is particularly important to emphasise your commitment and willingness to continue learning. This is obviously important if you are applying for a course or Apprenticeship, but also true if you are applying for any other type of work, as most jobs involve some amount of training.

Your qualifications

Listing your qualifications is the most obvious way of demonstrating to the selector that you have specific practical skills or knowledge of a particular subject, so it is very important that you present information about your qualifications accurately and effectively.

In the first instance, it may be useful to draw up a detailed list of all your qualifications that you can refer to whenever you apply for a job or course.

For each qualification, make a note of the:

- type of qualification (e.g. GCSE, Higher Diploma, Level 2 Award, A level, BTEC Level 3 National etc)

- subject

- grade

- date (the month and year you completed the course or took your final exams)

- units or modules taken as part of the qualification

- awarding body (e.g. Edexcel, AQA, City & Guilds etc).

Make sure you copy details precisely from any certificates you have already gained. Also, include details of any qualifications that you are currently working towards, plus their predicted grades (if available).

As well as qualifications gained at school or college, remember to include qualifications that you may have gained in other situations, such as first aid certificates, music qualifications, the Duke of Edinburgh's Award, certificates gained through a Young Enterprise programme, ASDAN Awards and so on.

When you come to apply for a job or course, refer back to this list to help you save time and to always present details about your qualifications accurately.

Overcoming problems

Finding a job or getting onto a college course isn't always straightforward. There are many different situations that may complicate matters for you and you may have to work that little bit harder to get what you want. There's always something you can do to improve your chances, so stay focused on your goal and see if there's someway you can work around the obstacles!

A lack of experience or skills

If you feel you don't measure up to what the selector is looking for, it's easy to feel put off from applying. As long as you at least tick some of the boxes, though, it may still be worth submitting an application. Make sure you demonstrate all your relevant qualities that **do** match the selection criteria and, if at all possible, avoid mentioning the ones that you are lacking (you don't want to highlight reasons to be rejected!). This is easily done on a CV, but you may find that an application form forces you to give evidence about how you meet all of the criteria. If this is the case, keep your answers simple and honest.

For example, if the criteria includes a particular type of experience that you lack, you may be able to say that:

- even though you don't have direct experience yourself, you have knowledge of what is required from observing someone else (from your work experience placement, for example)

- you have experience in a related area, which helped you develop relevant skills

- you have not yet had the opportunity to develop experience in this area, although you are very keen to do so as this is where your interests and ambitions lie.

Refer back to page 33 for information about transferable skills – the skills that you have developed from one area of your life that can be used in another situation. Remember, you may have more to offer than you think, and enthusiasm and a positive attitude can get you a long way!

A lack of qualifications

For some opportunities, if you don't have the required grades or qualifications, your application will be rejected automatically. However, selectors will often accept relevant experience in place of qualifications, if you can show that this has enabled you to gain the required expertise and knowledge. Usually, in this situation, selectors will be looking for a significant amount of relevant experience, such as a few years in a job or voluntary role.

If you are just starting out, however, you may not have the experience to compensate for a lack of qualifications. You will have to decide how best to approach this, depending on your situation.

- If you have no qualifications, use your covering letter to explain that, although you haven't done so well academically, you have other valuable qualities (such as practical skills, good people skills, etc).

- If you have some qualifications, but poor grades, it may be possible to list the subjects you have taken without giving details about your grades. For example, you might simply say, 'I have GCSEs in the following subjects . . . .'

If you failed to achieve the qualifications or grades you were expecting for reasons such as ill health or bereavement, selectors, particularly for college courses, may be able to take this into account. So, be prepared to explain your particular situation if you feel your final results are not a good reflection of your actual abilities.

The most important thing to remember is that you must be honest. Never change your grades or list qualifications you haven't got. If you're worried about listing poor results, speak to your local Connexions/careers service for advice about your particular situation.

Remember, there are many jobs that allow you to gain qualifications while you work, so whatever your situation, it is never too late to have another go.

Gaps

When it comes to completing an application form or writing your CV, you are usually expected to show that you have used your time constructively, whether by undertaking a course, paid employment, voluntary work or caring responsibilities. Selectors may assume the worst if there appears to be an unexplained gap in your education or employment dates.

For example, most selectors would overlook a gap of a month or two between finishing a course and starting a job, or even between two jobs. However, longer gaps may need an explanation. Selectors may worry that you were out of work for 'negative' reasons – you were sacked from your previous job, you were in prison, you lacked motivation or there was something about you that was making you 'unattractive' to other potential employers.

This can seem terribly unfair if you were unemployed due to circumstances beyond your control. If at all possible, show that you were still being constructive during this period – perhaps by undertaking voluntary work, unpaid work experience, short courses, or just by practising your skills in some way. Stay upbeat in your application; don't focus on being unemployed, but rather on the positive things you have to offer.

Gaps due to caring responsibilities (such as having a baby or caring for a disabled parent) are perfectly acceptable, so don't be afraid to state this as a reason for breaks in paid employment. There may be many useful, transferable skills that you have developed from these experiences, so make sure you highlight these as appropriate.

While it is increasingly common for young people to take a 'gap year' between leaving school and starting either university or a job, selectors will hope to see that the year was spent in a meaningful way, and wasn't just spent doing very little due to a lack of motivation. If you have taken a gap year, try to identify any transferable skills the experience helped you to develop.

Of course, the problem remains, how do you explain gaps in your education or employment history if they really were down to 'negative' reasons, such as prison, dismissal or lack of motivation? It's probably best to be honest, but brief – don't say more than you have to and don't blame others for the situation you found yourself in. Explain how you have:

- reflected on the experience
- learned something from it
- grown and changed as a person
- are now looking for the chance to make a positive contribution.

Chapter four

Understanding competencies

"I communicate well with people at all levels."

This chapter will help you:

- understand what competencies are
- understand why selectors use them
- demonstrate your competencies effectively.

You may hear employers referring to **competencies**, particularly as part of the recruitment process. Competencies represent a way of assessing the requirements of a particular job and deciding what a person needs to be able to do in order to be considered competent in that role. They may seem a little complicated to understand at first, but don't be put off if you see a vacancy referring to competencies; this chapter will help you understand how to deal with them.

Not all employers use competencies when they are recruiting. Some organisations may only choose to use them for more senior vacancies. Some smaller or more informal employers may not use them at all. However, being able to demonstrate that you are competent will be useful whichever type of organisation you apply to!

What are competencies?

As you will have seen from Chapter two, when a vacancy arises an employer will usually produce a job description setting out which tasks and responsibilities the role involves. Based on this job description, it is then possible to identify which **skills**, **knowledge** and **behaviours** are required to do the job effectively. Collectively, these may be referred to as competencies. It is becoming more common for selectors to ask applicants to show how they measure up to a range of competencies.

Some of the most frequently required competencies that employers look for include:

- communication skills
- teamworking
- customer service skills
- ability to deliver results
- problem-solving skills.

Employers may take this a stage further, and describe various levels of proficiency for each competency. For example, problem-solving skills may be categorised as follows:

Level 1 – uses judgement to assess nature of the problem; uses initiative to solve simple problems; seeks advice from supervisor for more complex problems.

Level 2 – identifies a range of possible solutions for complex problems; evaluates alternative solutions and makes recommendations to supervisor; agrees appropriate course of action with the supervisor before taking action.

Level 3 – takes responsibility for resolving the most complex problems; fully investigates causes and possible solutions; puts in place policies to prevent similar problems recurring; selects and implements action plans for preferred solutions.

Having decided which competencies are most relevant to the job, the employer will then use the application process (and, later, the interview stage) to find out whether applicants can demonstrate those competencies. You will be asked to give details of a real-life occasion in which you behaved in a way that shows the relevant competency. For example, to find out about an applicant's time management skills, an application form may include the question:

Describe an occasion when you had to deliver several pieces of work to a tight deadline. How did you manage your time?

Competency-based questions usually follow a similar structure; look out for those that start:

- Describe a situation when you...

- Give an example of how you...

- Provide details of an occasion when you...

These are just a few examples; others may be used, but in all cases you have the opportunity to prove you have a particular skill by showing how you have put it into action.

Why do selectors use competencies?

Competency-based application forms are popular with employers for a number of reasons.

- How you have behaved in the past is a good indication of how you will behave in the future! For example, if the employer asks about your teamworking skills, think about what your answer says about you. In a team, do you tend to take the lead, contribute in a supporting role, or let everyone else get on with it? We all have a tendency to behave in a certain way, which is what the employer is trying to find out.

- It would be easy for you to suggest that you have all sorts of different skills and aptitudes, but by asking for a real-life example, it becomes harder to bluff! Remember, if you are invited to an interview, you may be quizzed on any information that you have given in an application form, so you need to be honest.

- Competency-based questions give employers more meaningful information to base a decision on. For example, consider a job that requires good time-management skills. If you can show that, in the past, you have delivered several course assignments ahead of your deadlines by carefully organising your work, allowing extra time for unforeseen problems and being self-motivated to get the work done, this is more useful to an employer than just saying 'I have good time-management skills'!

- A competency-based application form forces all applicants to answer the same questions, making it easier for the employer to compare the skills of different candidates.

Another benefit, which may be relevant to you if you are just starting out in the job market, is that you don't need a lot of experience in the workplace in order to answer competency-based questions. Think of all the transferable skills you have built up through school or college work, volunteering, your home life, hobbies and activities, as well as through paid or unpaid work experience. These can all be used as examples in response to competency-based questions. Chapter three has more information about assessing your transferable skills, if you need a reminder about these.

Demonstrating your competencies

It is worth thinking carefully about how you answer competency-based questions on an application form. In each case:

- **give one specific, real-life situation** – identify a previous occasion when you demonstrated the relevant competency or skill

- **stress what actions you took** – discuss your own actions, emphasising what you did, rather than what other people did – but don't take credit for things you didn't do

- **give a concise response** – sticking to the most relevant facts

- **show self-awareness** – say what went well, but if things didn't all go according to plan, explain what lessons you learned and what you would do differently next time.

If there are several competency-based questions on the application form, choose different examples for each question, to show that you have a broad range of experience.

The CAR approach to competencies

A good way to structure your answers to competency-based questions is known as the CAR approach, which stands for context, action, results. Start by explaining briefly the background to the situation (the context), describe what you did (your actions) and finish by reflecting on the outcomes (the result).

Examples

Describe a situation when you used your initiative to solve a problem.

Context	When I worked for Hombell's Insurance company last summer, I noticed that it was hard to find things in their filing system.
Action	I came up with a way of reorganising the system and asked everyone in the office what they thought of it. Some of them suggested improvements to my original idea, so I had to revise my plans. I then worked out how much time it would take to reorganise the files, before passing on my recommendations to the manager.
Results	My manager agreed with my recommendations and asked me to update the filing system according to my plans. It took two weeks to reorganise it, but it's been estimated that the new system saves each worker around 15 minutes a day. By asking for other people's ideas, the new system is much easier to use and takes into account everyone's different requirements.

Give an example of a time when you were involved in organising an event or project.

Context	I am a member of the drama society at college. We staged a play during the summer that was set in Victorian times. I was in charge of the team responsible for finding, hiring, making and altering the costumes.
Action	I began by making a plan of what needed to be done and by when. At our first meeting, I asked for volunteers to take on different tasks and got people to agree deadlines for getting things done. I made notes of everything that we agreed and made sure we all were clear about what was required. I organised regular sessions so that we could meet and work together on fittings, alterations and so on. We had a lot to do, so it was important for me to keep everyone motivated and also to keep the director up to date with our progress.

Results	The team worked really well together and all of the costumes looked great on the night! I think that by coming up with a plan from the start it was easy to monitor our progress and organise more frequent sessions when it looked like we might fall behind.

How competent are you?

Think about how you would demonstrate some of the more common competencies that employers look for. Sketch out a table, as shown below, and use the CAR approach to structure your answers.

Competency	Context	Action	Result
Using your initiative			
Team working			
Verbal communication			
Time management			
Problem solving			
Organising			
Customer service			
Coping with pressure			
Leadership			
Written communication			
Delivering results			

You may find that you have strengths in some areas, but are weaker in others. If that is the case, consider getting involved in new activities or putting yourself forward for positions of responsibility wherever possible, so that you can more easily demonstrate a good range of skills and competencies. Demonstrating your competencies may seem daunting at first, but as you gain experience in the workplace, you will find that it becomes much easier!

Chapter five

CVs: getting started

"I'm trying to cut my CV down to 140 characters to put it on Twitter..."

This chapter will:

- help you understand what a CV is and why you need one
- explain exactly what information you need to include on your CV
- show you how you can write a CV that works for you
- make you aware of the dangers of giving out too much information.

What is a CV?

The term CV is an abbreviation for curriculum vitae, which means 'the course of your life'. Sometimes CVs are called résumés (although this is an American term). A CV is basically a document that gives a brief overview of your skills, qualifications and experience.

CVs are only used to apply for jobs, not courses. When making job applications, you may use your CV in different ways. You could:

- email it to prospective employers on spec
- send it with a covering letter to apply for an advertised vacancy, where a CV has been requested
- send it to a recruitment agency
- upload it onto a website.

Your CV is a very useful document that you'll need to update as you progress through your career. It's also an excellent reference sheet that you can use when you're filling in application forms (for details of your qualifications, dates etc) or to help you prepare for an interview. Re-reading your CV before an interview can help you think about your past experiences and achievements, and the skills you've gained.

Having a great CV is important. Submitting your CV is often the first opportunity you'll have to make a good impression on potential employers. It's estimated that many busy employers spend only 30 seconds looking at a CV before they make a decision about your application. Your CV gives a potential employer a snapshot of your skills, abilities and strengths and if it impresses the employer, you may well be asked to an interview. That's why your CV needs to be great!

Frequently asked questions

What makes a great CV?

Everyone has a different idea about what makes a great CV. However, there are some golden rules that you need to stick to.

- Make it clear and concise. Don't write ten pages about your skills, keep it easy to read and well structured.
- Be accurate and honest. Don't lie or get the names of your qualifications wrong!
- Make sure it's well presented. Your CV should be wordprocessed, using a clear font and free of mistakes.

There are two main styles of CV, chronological and functional. Chronological CVs present information in reverse date order (the most recent information is shown first). Functional CVs (sometimes known as skills based) emphasise an applicant's skills, rather than guiding the reader through their history in date order. These two styles are described in more detail in the next chapter.

You may want to adapt your CV for a particular job. When you are writing your CV, you need to consider which style is right for the position you're applying for. Chapter six has advice on choosing which style of CV to use. You can also look at examples of CVs in Chapter seven.

There is no single right CV style, but the following chapters have lots of clear advice on exactly what information to include on your CV and how to present it.

What are employers looking for on a CV?

When an employer receives a CV they are looking to see how it matches their selection criteria. Chapter two has some useful advice to help you understand the recruitment process and identify the skills that employers are looking for. The employer may have very specific criteria in mind, a qualification in sport or customer service skills, for example. The easier you can make it for an employer to scan your CV and pick out relevant information, the greater your chance of success.

How long should my CV be?

Your CV is meant to give an employer a taste of your skills and achievements; it isn't supposed to tell them your life history! Ideally, it shouldn't be any longer than two sides of A4.

Don't try to 'pad out' your CV either; if it's only one side of A4, don't worry – as long as you've said everything about yourself that is relevant. As long as you've included all the important information an employer needs, don't be tempted to fill up space.

Why is it important to be accurate and honest?

When you're writing your CV you may be tempted to 'up' a couple of your qualification grades, or talk up any responsibilities you've had in a job. Don't!

It's important to be honest when you're applying for a job for a number of reasons. For one, you can be dismissed if you're found to have lied during the application process. Many employers check facts such as qualifications (they may ask you to bring in your certificates) and responsibilities held in previous positions (by contacting referees). Lying on your CV is likely to effectively end your relationship with that employer if you're found out. Be honest – if you haven't got as many qualifications as you'd like, but you're motivated and would be happy to try and gain more, say it. Many employers will welcome an applicant who is willing to work towards further qualifications.

Before you start writing

Before you start writing your CV you need to gather all your information together. To make sure that your CV is as accurate as possible, it's worth double checking the following facts.

Qualification names and grades. When you list your qualifications it's important to use the correct name for each one. To find these out, you can check what's written on your exam certificates (if you've already received them). Or, if you're still studying, you could speak to your teacher/tutor or personal/careers adviser who may be able to check this for you. The same goes for your grades; if you've already achieved a particular grade, make sure you record this on your CV accurately. If you haven't finished your course yet, you can include your predicted grades.

Dates. When did you complete a particular course? When did you do your work experience? If you've got a part-time job – when did you start? Don't just guess; if you're not sure, check your dates. You don't need to be too specific, but you do need to list the correct month and year.

Spelling of names. If you mention any businesses or organisations on your CV, including voluntary groups, social clubs or sports teams, you need to check how to spell their names. It might sound like an unnecessary check but it pays to be sure. Misspellings can make a potential employer think you're careless.

What do you need to include on your CV?

In the next chapter, you'll be introduced to the different ways of presenting your CV. However, no matter which style you choose, you will need to make sure that your CV has all the vital information about you that prospective employers need, including:

- your contact details
- your education and qualifications
- any training you've done
- your work experience/career history.

The headings listed below describe the information that you'll need to include on your CV. Depending on the style of CV you choose, you may or may not want to include a personal profile or a skills/achievements section.

Contact details

The first section of information on your CV is your contact details, including your name, address, telephone number and email address. Most people put this information at the very top of the first page of their CV. Depending on the style of your CV, you may want to centralise this information, so it's easy for the reader to spot. Below is an example of how you could set this out.

James Boxford
21 Avenue Road, Old Town
Shireford HS23 2DJ
01223 554633 / 0876 676908
james@sampleemail.com

You can include your home phone number and mobile number, or just your mobile, whichever you feel makes it easiest for employers to contact you. If you give your home number out, it's worth telling your parents/ family, so that if an employer rings and you're not available, anyone answering the phone knows what the call is about.

When you've finished your CV it's worth double checking that you've written your mobile number correctly. It's very easy to mistype a long number; one digit wrong may make the different between receiving a phone call inviting you to interview, and not!

Any email address you list on your CV needs to be appropriate for work use. Addresses such as partygirl@greenmail.com might seem funny with your friends, but it won't make a good impression on a potential employer. If necessary, set up a new email account, with a sensible name (your surname and some numbers are a good choice). If you do set up a new email account, check it works before giving out the address!

Education and qualifications

Under this heading, you need to list the school(s) and college(s) you attended, the dates you started and left, and the qualifications you achieved (including your grades). You should list qualifications in the order that you gained them, starting with the most recent.

- Don't include details of your primary school.

- Don't give the whole address of your secondary school or college; just the name and town is enough.

- Remember to be consistent in the way you present information e.g. list the school/college name, then qualification, subject and finally grade.

As a general rule, the higher up the educational ladder you go, the less you need to mention lower-level qualifications, so if you have five GCSEs mention each one separately including the grades you achieved. Someone with a degree however, wouldn't need to list their GCSEs.

Here is an example of how you could list your qualifications.

September 2008 – June 2010 Westlee College, Old Town
A levels in English (grade B), art (grade A) and history (grade C).

September 2003 – June 2008 St Mary's School, Old Town
Eight GCSEs at grades A*-C including English, science and maths.

Lots of employers look for applicants with GCSEs in English, maths and science, so if you have any/all of these subjects it's worth mentioning them (as in the example above) even if you aren't listing your other subjects.

If any of the qualifications you achieved were made up of units or modules, it may be worth listing the units/modules you studied. This is particularly important if some of the units you studied are of direct relevance to the position you are applying for. It may also be the case that the title of the qualification doesn't explain the extent of your studies; for example on a business studies course you may also study modules on marketing, economics, human resources and business law. If the units are relevant, make sure you list them on your CV. Here is an example of how you could do this.

> **September 2009 – June 2010 BTEC Level 2 Diploma in animal care (Merit).**
> During this course I completed the following modules:
>
> - maintain animal accommodation
>
> - maintain animal health and welfare
>
> - undertake practical animal feeding
>
> - introduction to how the principles and practices of animal behaviour and handling contribute to the nursing of animals
>
> - understand the basic principles of animal biology.

If you achieved poor grades in some of your qualifications and you're not sure how to present this information, see page 40 for advice.

Work experience/career history

In this section you need to list any jobs you've had. You might not have had much experience of employment, but that's fine. Perhaps you've had a Saturday job or a holiday job; these are certainly worth mentioning as you will have gained useful skills and experience. You can also list any work experience placements and if relevant to what you're applying for, describe what you did/learned. If you've taken part in any voluntary work, make sure you mention this too.

If you've had more than one job, mention your most recent (or current) position first. If the position was voluntary, make it clear you were a volunteer. For each position you need to include the following information.

- Dates – the month and year you started and finished. For work experience placements, include the length of the placement, e.g. one week.

- Your job title.

- The name of the company or organisation you worked for.

- A brief description of your role and key duties/responsibilities.

The exact order that you give the information is up to you, you might want to list your job title first, or the employer's name. Below is an example of how this information could be set out.

> **June 2009 – July 2010 Waitress, Trish's Tea Rooms, Shireford.**
> My duties included greeting customers and showing them to their table, taking orders, serving food and drinks, clearing tables and helping out in the kitchen as required.

Your experience can provide proof of your skills and personal qualities, which prospective employers are very interested in. It's worth taking your time getting this section right.

Training

If you have completed any training courses, this is the place to mention them. Perhaps you've done a short course in ICT, photography or food hygiene or even completed a course with your employer (if you have a job) or as part of a voluntary scheme. Any, or all of these, are likely to be of interest to a potential employer.

Here are some tips about presenting training information.

- List your courses in a sensible order – you could list the most relevant to the job first, or in date order.

- If the course title doesn't make it clear what the course was about, include a brief summary (a sentence or two at the most) of what you learned.

- State where you did the course, but don't put the whole address, simply 'Cambridge Regional College' or 'Timeworks, London' will do.

Some training may have no direct relevance to the job you are applying for, but it may highlight the range of skills and knowledge you have that will be useful for the work. If so, try to spell this out, perhaps in the 'Additional information' section described later, or the reader may not understand the point.

Remember that many skills are transferable, so any training you've done may well be relevant to a different area of work. For example, suppose you worked in a shop and the company sent you on a customer service course. The skills you learned on that course would be just as valuable if you became a sales representative, a customer services manager, or worked in a different type of shop, or anywhere else where you have direct contact with customers or the public. See Chapter three for more information about transferable skills.

Information you may want to include

It's entirely up to you whether or not you decide to include the type of information listed below. The following sections can give you the opportunity to mention any experiences, hobbies, skills or interests that you think will be relevant to the position you're interested in. You may choose to include the following information on your CV:

- personal profile
- skills/achievements
- leisure interests
- additional information
- referees.

Personal profile

A personal profile is a piece of text that aims to sell you and your skills to an employer. It's your opportunity to 'pitch' yourself! The profile should be no longer than two or three sentences and should give the reader a brief summary about you, your qualities, strengths and skills. You can also include a sentence about the type of role you are looking for.

If you find it difficult to write about your strengths, you may be tempted not to include a personal profile on your CV. But, there are a couple of reasons why you might chose to include one. Firstly, you can use your personal profile to emphasise any skills or personal qualities you have that are essential for the job you are interested in. For example, if you're applying for a job as a veterinary nurse, you could write about your caring skills. Secondly, you can use your personal profile to tell an employer about you, not just your qualifications; this can really give your CV some personality, and can allow an employer to judge whether or not you'll fit in with the rest of the team.

Skills/achievements

You may want to list your achievements and the skills you have that relate to the position you are applying for. A good way of doing this is a bulleted list, which states the skill and includes an example of when you have demonstrated that skill. For example:

> **Communication skills.** During the past six months I have worked in the busy high street fashion store, Looks, and feel I am able to communicate effectively with customers. I have dealt successfully with queries and complaints and am confident when speaking to customers.

This section is particularly important if you want to submit a functional or skills-based CV, which emphasises the relevant skills you have, rather than your qualifications. For more information about functional CVs, see Chapter six.

Some people don't include a skills and achievements heading, and instead mention relevant skills in their personal profile.

Leisure interests

You can use this heading to write about any leisure interests you have. You could mention if you are a member of a club, your involvement with a charity or fundraising organisation or if you've taken part in the Duke of Edinburgh's Award programme or similar.

Don't just list your information; think instead about what qualities these activities demanded. You could mention the skills you've developed through these activities. Some examples are given below.

- Membership of a club can indicate that you are a sociable person, or that you have a particular skill or talent. It also shows that you are motivated and committed.

- Extra responsibilities at school or college (for example, being a prefect) show that you are reliable, trustworthy and responsible. You also need organisational skills to take on extra responsibilities.

- Duke of Edinburgh's Award shows determination, reliability and willingness to work hard. You may have developed teamwork and problem-solving skills.

You should only list genuine interests and hobbies. For example, don't say you enjoy running marathons if you've never attempted one. An interviewer may ask you about anything you've written on your CV, so don't get caught out!

Additional information

This is a useful heading to use if you want to mention anything else that you feel is relevant to the position you are interested in.

Additional information that may well interest a prospective employer could include:

- extra responsibilities you've had at school or college
- any language skills you have
- if you have a driving licence.

If you've been fortunate enough to have something published, no matter how modest the publication, do mention it if it's relevant to the position you're applying for. Have you designed web pages, written an information leaflet, edited the school magazine? If any relate directly to the type of work you are applying for, you may want to send a copy or give a brief description.

If you don't have much work experience then providing this type of information to prospective employers, as proof of your abilities, is especially important.

Referees

You can list your referees and their contact details under this heading, or you can leave their details out and simply add the phrase 'References available on request'. Neither option is wrong – the choice is yours!

If you are going to list details of your referees on your CV, for each one you will need to state their name, address and telephone number. You only need to give a maximum of two referees. Obviously, if you have had a previous job, one of your referees should be your previous manager. If you have not had a previous job you could ask:

- a teacher from school or a lecturer from college
- a professional person or youth worker who knows you well
- the coach or leader of a club you belong to.

Choose your referees carefully. You should select people who you feel have a good opinion of you, and who know something about your skills or experiences. **Always check with referees that they are happy to provide a reference, and are prepared to be listed on your CV, before including them on your CV.**

Some people don't list their referees, perhaps because they haven't decided who to ask for a reference, or because they are sending a CV on spec and don't feel it's necessary. This is completely acceptable as any prospective employer can ask you for details of referees later on in the recruitment process.

What to leave out

The start of this chapter described all the information you should include on your CV. However, there are also some personal details and information that you definitely should not include; the following are examples.

Date of birth

Until recently, it was common to include your date of birth on your CV, but this is no longer the case. It's unnecessary. Anti-discrimination legislation also means that it's unlawful for an employer to discriminate against a candidate on the basis of their age, so you should not feel obliged to provide it.

Photo

Unless you are applying for work as a model or an actor, there is absolutely no need to attach a photo of yourself to your CV. Employers are interested in your skills and abilities, not what you look like.

National Insurance number

You should be very careful who you give your National Insurance (NI) number to as it can be used to steal your identity. Only give your NI number to trusted officials who need it, such as your employer's human resources department, once you have been offered a job. **Never** include your NI number on your CV.

The risk of identity theft

When you've written your CV you need to be aware how your information might be used when it's out of your hands. Identity theft is on the rise, and making your personal details, such as your date of birth, address and National Insurance number, widely available makes it very easy for someone else to steal your identity. To minimise the risk of this happening to you, don't include your personal details (date of birth or NI number) on your CV and think about the following.

Who are you sending your CV to?

Doing some research on the company you would like to work for has many advantages, one of which is that you can be sure that you're sending your CV to a genuine organisation. If you are thinking of applying to a company that you are completely unfamiliar with, you could use the phone book, local directories and the internet to check that the company exists and that any contact details are correct.

Posting your CV online

Posting your CV online may make it more available to employers, but it'll also make your details more available to the wrong people. If you want to post your CV online you should remove some of your personal details (such as address and telephone number).

Making your CV work for you

If you want to maximise your chances of success, sending out the same CV for every vacancy you're interested in isn't a great idea. You need to adapt your CV so that it meets the needs of the particular job that you are applying for.

If you're replying to a job advert

If you are sending your CV in response to a job advert, employers will judge your application against their selection criteria; candidates who don't meet the criteria won't be shortlisted. So, it makes sense to find out as much as you can about the position you're interested in, and what the employer is looking for, and then use this information to make your CV stand out!

Chapter two has some great advice on how to identify what employers want.

Adapting your CV for each position you apply for doesn't have to be a mammoth task. Keep an electronic copy of your CV, and when you need to adapt it, save another copy under a different name to work on.

If you choose to send out the same CV to every job vacancy, you risk employers passing you by because you haven't sold yourself in the best possible way.

If you're sending your CV on spec

Even if you're sending your CV on spec, you can still do some research to find out what types of skills you will need for the job you are interested in. These are the skills that potential employers will be looking for.

When you know what employers are likely to want, you can tailor your CV to these requirements. For example, if you decide to send your CV on spec to several hairdressing salons in your area, you could do some research into the skills and qualities that are needed for this type of work. You could then submit a functional CV that includes examples of how you've demonstrated each of these skills.

Speak to your local Connexions/careers centre to get help researching particular careers. The *Jobs4u* website also has a lot of useful information, see: www.connexions-direct.com/jobs4u/index.cfm.

If you are sending your CV on spec to several employers for the same type of job, it would be fine to use just one CV.

When you've finished

When you've finished writing your CV, you will need to proofread it for typos, spelling and grammatical errors. It is easy not to notice any mistakes on screen, so it's always better to check a printout if possible. Try reading what you've written aloud. When you're typing it's easy to leave small words out – errors like this are simpler to spot if you read what you've written aloud.

- Try not to check your CV as soon as you've written it. You're more likely to spot errors if you've not read the document recently; even a few hours can help.

- Check your spelling. Using the wrong word (e.g. their and there are often misuscd) will make your CV look unprofessional – if you're not sure which spelling to use, look it up!

- Make sure the language on your spell checker is set to English (UK) and not English (US).

Double check your contact details including your phone number and email address.

It's hard to proofread your own work, so ask someone else to check your CV for errors as well.

If you're having problems

Writing your CV can be tricky and if you're struggling there are lots of people who will be able to help you. Your first step should be to get in touch with your local Connexions or careers service. If you're still at school or college, you may have a careers adviser or coordinator that you can speak to.

You may prefer to speak to a friend or relative about your CV. It's certainly useful to have someone read over your CV and check for spelling and grammatical errors. However, if someone suggests altering your CV considerably and you're not sure if their advice is correct, try to speak to a personal/careers adviser about the issue. Everyone has an opinion on what makes a good CV, but not everyone is right!

If you apply for a job, but aren't shortlisted, it might be worth asking the recruiter for some feedback on your CV. Feedback from employers is often useful and could help you improve your CV for your next application.

Chapter six

CVs: styles

"I know it's unusual but I'd like to present my cv in the form of contemporary dance."

This chapter will:

- describe the most popular styles of CV
- help you decide which style is best for you
- answer some FAQs about presenting information.

There are lots of different ways of setting out the information on your CV. Despite what you might hear, there is no single 'correct' way to do this. There are hundreds of different opinions on how a CV should be laid out and recruiters all have different expectations. The most important thing to remember is that your CV needs to be well presented, easy to read and right for the job you are applying for. You need to choose a style that makes it easy for the recruiting manager to identify the information on your CV that is most relevant to the position you are interested in.

When you're writing your CV you need to think about the following points.

- What do you think the employer is most interested in?
- What's the most important/relevant information on your CV and how can you make it stand out?

The styles below are a good starting point. However, feel free to change the structure when you need to – as long as you've included all the vital information an employer needs (see Chapter five about what to include). As a general rule, list the most important and most relevant information first.

The two most popular CV styles are:

- chronological
- functional or skills based.

Chronological CVs

As the name suggests, a chronological CV presents material in chronological (date) order. Information is usually presented in reverse order – that is, the most recent information is shown first. The chronological CV takes the reader step by step through your education history, then your work history, and finally, to your additional information. You can see an example of a chronological CV in Chapter seven.

Chronological CVs may include the following information; think about which headings are appropriate for your CV.

Contact details – including your name, address, telephone numbers and email address.

Personal profile – a short paragraph selling your skills and strengths to the reader (this is optional; some people choose not to include this information).

Education – names of schools and dates attended, details of qualifications and grades achieved.

Training – details of any training courses you've attended.

Career to date – dates, name and address of employer, job title and responsibilities.

Additional information – details of any other experience that might be of interest to an employer.

Leisure interests – details of your hobbies, membership of a club or involvement with a charity.

References.

Some people choose to change the order of this information. As mentioned in the previous chapter, some of these headings are optional, and you may choose not to include them – perhaps because you don't feel you have anything relevant to say.

 In some instances you may want to list your career to date before your education details. If you have just left education, however, you may want to list your qualifications first. The great thing about CVs is that there is no one, right way.

Advantages of chronological CVs

- They are easy to put together.

- The style makes it straightforward to update content in future.

- Employers can get a clear idea of your progression through education and work.

Functional (or skills-based) CVs

The purpose of this style is to focus the reader's attention on the skills you have, which are relevant for the job. These might be skills that you've developed through school, college or university, part-time work, voluntary work or even a hobby. Whatever your skills, you need to present them in a punchy and eye-catching way; they are the main emphasis of this style. On a functional CV other sections of information are often kept brief.

When listing skills on your CV, you should include an example of how you have demonstrated each skill, as evidence of your abilities. You could consider using the CAR approach for this (see Chapter four for more information). Where possible, it's also useful to give the reader an idea of your level of skill. For example, instead of saying you have practical skills, give specific examples, such as 'I can use different tools including drills, planes and sanders safely, and am able to do simple DIY jobs such as putting up shelves and fitting curtain poles'.

This is an increasingly popular form of CV presentation, although it does require that you already have relevant skills or you'll find it difficult to write! You can see an example of a functional CV in Chapter seven.

Functional CVs may include the following information; think about which headings are appropriate for your CV.

Contact details – including your name, address, telephone numbers and email address.

Personal profile – a short paragraph selling yourself to the reader.

Skills – list your skills (one bullet point per skill) with a clear example of how you've demonstrated that skill.

Key achievements – this should be a list of your achievements – try to be specific, such as 'I arranged a staff party, which involved hiring a venue, caterers and a dj and working to a budget'.

Education and training – brief details only, showing key qualifications, courses and dates.

Career history – again, list brief details only: for each job include your employer's name, the dates of employment, your job title and a very brief description of your role.

Additional information

Referees

As with the chronological style of CV, some of the headings mentioned above are optional and you may choose not to include them. You can also change the order of the headings to suit your needs.

You may need to adapt the style to suit your needs. For example, perhaps you can't think of many key achievements that you could list, in which case you could leave that heading out. People with lots of experience and examples of their achievements may choose to use the entire first page of their CV listing these, with all other details only listed briefly.

Advantages of functional CVs

- If you don't have many qualifications (or low grades) this layout allows you to emphasise your skills instead.

- If you've had a few, very different jobs, this type of CV can allow you to emphasise all the transferable skills you've built up and present your career history in a positive way.

- Once you've had one or more jobs that relate to the position you are interested in, a functional CV allows you to present all the relevant skills you've developed together in one combined list, making it easy for employers to see a summary of your abilities.

Targeting your CV to each vacancy

However tempting it may be to write one CV and use that for all your applications, don't! Your CV is often the first chance you'll get to make an impression on an employer. CVs that don't present information in a direct and relevant way may well end up on the rejection pile.

The best approach is to make sure the CV you send out is tailored to the particular vacancy you are applying for. However, if you are sending your CV on spec to different employers, but looking for the same type of job, it would be appropriate to use the same CV.

You could adapt your CV in the following ways.

If a job requires particular qualifications that you have, you could list these first to catch the reader's eye.

If a job requires certain experience that you have, you could move this section to the top of your CV and add some more detail about your experiences, what you learned and how it developed your skills.

If a job requires particular skills, but not many qualifications, you could expand the skills section of your CV, with more examples of how you've demonstrated these skills. You could also summarise your qualifications, rather than listing them separately.

In order to target your CV, you'll need to read the job advert, job description and person specification carefully. Chapter two has more advice about identifying what employers are looking for.

FAQs about presenting your information

Which fonts should I use?

Choose a font that is clear, easy to read and not too unusual. Times New Roman, Arial and Verdana all work well. Try to use only one or two fonts

– anymore can make a document look messy. The font size should be easy to read, ideally point 10 or 12. You can use a larger size for headings.

It's also worth remembering that if you choose to email your CV, any unusual fonts you've used in your document might not be recognised by a potential employer's computer.

Should I use lots of formatting?

You want your CV to look clear, professional and well presented, but you don't necessarily need lots of formatting to do this. Unless you're very confident of your design skills, it's best to avoid using lots of italics, underlining or shading as these can make a document look cluttered and difficult to read.

- Separate sections with white space, so that text does not look cramped; double spacing between paragraphs works well.
- Leave a good margin around your text, about 25mm.
- Be consistent – make sure any spaces you leave between sections are of equal size.

How should I format headings?

Keep the headings simple but make them stand out – use bold, italic or a larger font size. You could also use upper case letters or a slightly different font. Whatever you choose to do, make sure you are consistent and all of your headings are presented in the same way.

Should I title my CV 'Curriculum Vitae'?

This is really a matter of personal choice. Many people feel that it is unnecessary to write the words curriculum vitae at the top of their CV, as it is obvious to the reader what the document is. However it isn't wrong, so if you want to do this, go ahead. A good alternative is to use your name as the 'title' of the document, perhaps by writing it in a larger font, and centralising it at the very top of the page.

Can I use bullet points?

Yes. Bullet points can catch the reader's attention and can allow you to summarise key information clearly and concisely. Don't go overboard though; you don't need to put all your information into bullet points.

Is it OK to use a CV template?

There are a lot of websites that allow you to download CV templates, usually for free. Many wordprocessing packages also offer you the option of compiling your CV using standard templates. If you don't know where to start, these can be useful. However, there are a few points that you should bear in mind.

- With some templates it's not possible to change headings or the order of the headings. This can be a problem as you may not be able to customise your CV as you'd like.

- Check out which fonts the template includes. If you're emailing your CV, as mentioned above, any unusual fonts you use may not be recognised by an employer's computer.

- If you're using the internet to find CV templates, steer clear of American sites, which may use different terms and conventions to UK sites.

- One other thing to bear in mind is that some CV templates may be very popular. If you want your CV to stand out, using the same template as everyone else isn't a great idea.

Despite the points mentioned above, templates can be a really useful tool. Lots of recruitment websites have free templates. It's also worth speaking to your local Connexions/careers service and checking out their websites, some of which have CV templates that you can download. You can also look at the CV examples given in Chapter seven, and use these to create your own template.

Points to remember

- The styles given in this chapter are only suggestions; you can amend them as you feel necessary.

- Whichever style you use, present the most important and most relevant information first.

- Look at your CV from the perspective of a potential employer; is it easy to see the information that's most relevant to your application?

- The great thing about CV styles is there is no right or wrong. The right CV for you will be the one that tells an employer clearly about the skills and experience you have that are relevant to the role. The exact style you use is up to you.

Chapter seven

CVs: examples

This chapter will:

- show you some examples of CVs
- give you some ideas of how to lay out your information.

If you've already read Chapter six you will know that there isn't one correct style of CV. The key to a good CV layout is presenting your information in a clear and concise way. The layout should help the selector identify the key points on your CV easily. This chapter includes examples of both chronological and functional CVs.

Chronological CVs

- Philipa is sending her CV on spec to local employers. Philipa has relevant experience that she gained as a volunteer, which she hopes employers will be interested in.

- Chris is sending his CV in response to a job advert – he has picked out the qualities the employer is looking for (from the job advert) and mentions these in his personal profile.

- Amir is also sending his CV in response to a job advert; the main focus of his CV is his education and qualifications section, as the employer is looking for a candidate with scientific qualifications.

Functional CVs

- Rosie is sending her CV on spec. She highlights skills that she feels would interest potential employers.

- Keisha is also sending her CV on spec. She uses her work experience and hobbies to demonstrate the skills she has that would be useful for the career she's interested in.

- Kevin is sending his CV to an employer to apply for a job. As the job he is interested in requires particular skills, rather than qualifications, Kevin lists these first.

Chronological CVs

The first CV belongs to Philipa who has just left college and is looking for a junior position with a website design company. She is sending this chronological CV on spec to several local companies that employ designers.

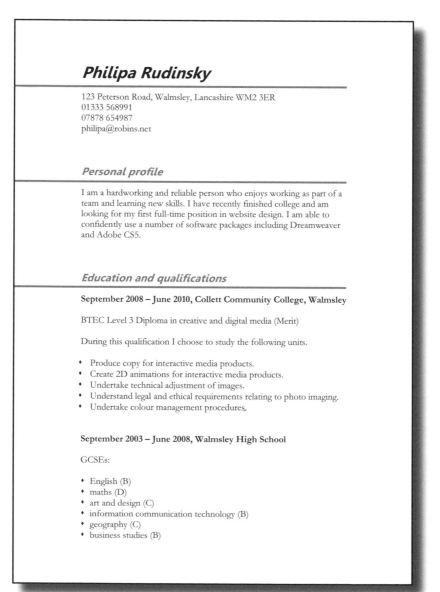

Philipa Rudinsky

123 Peterson Road, Walmsley, Lancashire WM2 3ER
01333 568991
07878 654987
philipa@robins.net

Personal profile

I am a hardworking and reliable person who enjoys working as part of a team and learning new skills. I have recently finished college and am looking for my first full-time position in website design. I am able to confidently use a number of software packages including Dreamweaver and Adobe CS5.

Education and qualifications

September 2008 – June 2010, Collett Community College, Walmsley

BTEC Level 3 Diploma in creative and digital media (Merit)

During this qualification I choose to study the following units.

- Produce copy for interactive media products.
- Create 2D animations for interactive media products.
- Undertake technical adjustment of images.
- Understand legal and ethical requirements relating to photo imaging.
- Undertake colour management procedures.

September 2003 – June 2008, Walmsley High School

GCSEs:

- English (B)
- maths (D)
- art and design (C)
- information communication technology (B)
- geography (C)
- business studies (B)

Career to date

October 2008 – present, volunteer with Walmsley Helpers

Walmsley Helpers is a charity that gives young people the chance to get involved in community projects. I started by taking part in projects, such as redecorating the community centre, but am now involved in organising and promoting projects. My main role is assisting the group leader develop their website www.warmsleyhelpers.co.uk. This involves:

* identifying which projects to promote on the site
* building pages for each upcoming activity, using photos
* linking each project to a registration page, so volunteers can apply to take part
* writing text for the website
* liaising with local schools and youth groups, to organise links between our websites.

October 2007 – Work experience at Prestige Developers

I spent a week at Prestige Developers, a website design company, during Year 11. I sat in on meetings with clients and learned about the importance of understanding your target audience. I shadowed a designer who was working on a brief for a local restaurant and helped test the new site.

July 2008 – July 2010, NAS Newsagents, Walmsley

I worked at NAS Newsagents on Saturdays and my duties included handling money, dealing with customers, sorting out paper bills and filling shelves with stock.

Other information

I enjoy photography and often act as 'official' photographer at parties and family gatherings. I have been complimented on my creative images, which I have produced using Photoshop.

Philipa Rudinsky   07878 654987   philipa@robins.net

The next chronological CV belongs to Chris who is applying for an assistant position at the Museum of Local History. The Museum is looking for a friendly, extrovert person to assist members of the public and provide information in a busy environment. The advert also states that experience of dealing with members of the public and some knowledge of local history would be an advantage. As Chris has these requirements, he mentions them in his personal profile, at the start of his CV.

Chris Whitman
22 Victoria Street, Broadtown BD1 4AL
Tel: 01999 692874
Email: chrisw@example.net

Personal profile:	I am a reliable and enthusiastic worker and enjoy dealing with members of the public. Although a team player (I am a member of a local football team), I also work well on my own initiative. I enjoy learning about history and regularly attend talks organised by Broadtown History Club.
Employment:	**August 2009 – present:** Picture-it camera shop. Full-time retail assistant. The job involves sales work, displaying new stock and dealing with customers' enquiries. **September 2008 – July 2009:** The Old Crown pub and restaurant. Part-time waiter. **October 2008:** Work experience. Broadtown Leisure Centre. Handled customers' enquiries, via telephone and in person, updated booking database for sports facilities and helped to promote a new aerobics class.
Education:	**Broadtown Comprehensive School, 2004-2009** GCSEs gained: • History A • Art and design C • French B • Design and technology C • English C • Mathematics D • Science D
Interests:	**Football** – I have played for a local team for the past two years and enjoy keeping fit. **Member of Broadtown History Club** – I enjoy attending lectures and researching local places of interest.
Referees:	The names of two referees can be supplied on request.

The next chronological CV belongs to Amir who is applying for a job as a lab technician. The employer is looking for a candidate with good A levels (or equivalent) in science subjects, who is reliable, and can pay attention to detail. As Amir has a relevant qualification, he lists this first; Amir also lists the units that he studied during his BTEC to show the extent of his studies. Although he does not have relevant work experience, Amir uses his work experience at the farm shop to demonstrate his relevant qualities.

Amir Begum

15 Park Close, South Town SJ21 5JC.
Email: a.begum@anymail.com
Telephone: 0721 923 384

EDUCATION AND QUALIFICATIONS

2008 – 2010	**South Town College**

BTEC Level 3 Diploma in Applied Science (Pass) – units included:

- fundamentals of science
- working in the science industry
- scientific practical techniques
- using science in the workplace
- chemical laboratory techniques
- practical chemical analysis
- medical physics techniques
- biochemical techniques
- genetics and genetic engineering.

2003 – 2008   **South Town School**
GCSEs in: maths (B), English (B), chemistry (C), biology (C), physics (C), geography (C), music (A) and physical education (B).

WORK EXPERIENCE

July 2008 – current   **Part-time sales assistant, South Town Organic Farm Shop**
Duties include:

- Taking delivery of fresh produce – I am reliable and always meet the delivery driver at the shop before it opens. I have to be there on time in order to ensure that stock is on display, ready for customers.

- Updating stock lists and unpacking goods – I work carefully and always double check my lists to ensure that they are accurate.

- Assembling crates for the home-delivery service – this involves paying close attention to detail and following instructions carefully as I only select items that the customer has agreed in advance.

INTERESTS

I enjoy playing cricket and am a member of South Town Under 21's Cricket Team. I also help coach the Under 10's team every Wednesday evening. As both coaching and playing cricket involve a regular commitment, I feel this demonstrates that I am reliable and responsible.

REFERENCES

Mrs C Reed, Manager, South Town Organic Farm Shop, Bramble Lane, South Town SJ21 3ER. Telephone: 01555 010101. Email: c.reed@anymail.com

Mr J Philips, Chairman, South Town Cricket Club, Redmore Road, South Town SJ21 8EH. Telephone: 01555 282828. Email: r.philips@anymail.com

Functional CVs

The first functional CV belongs to Rosie who has some work experience but is looking to move on to a more senior role. Rosie emphasises the strongest element of her CV first, i.e her experience; she then uses examples to illustrate her skills. Rosie sends this CV on spec to theatre companies which she feels she may like to work for.

ROSIE JONES

15 Kent Road, Eastborough EB8 9BL.
Tel: 01555 888888
Mobile: 07879 111111
Email: rosiejones@example.com

PERSONAL PROFILE

I am a highly motivated and efficient administrator with experience of delivering marketing campaigns. I have excellent ICT, communication and teamworking skills. Having recently trained two new members of staff, I have also demonstrated an aptitude for managing and motivating others. Keen to progress to a marketing role within a theatre company, I am eager to take on more responsibilities.

EMPLOYMENT HISTORY

August 2009 – present: The Creative Theatre Company. Arts administrator.

My duties include:

- helping to arrange performances at local schools and theatres
- writing publicity materials including e-flyers, direct mail and adverts
- responding to queries from suppliers, performers and the public
- arranging for the printing of brochures, posters and tickets
- coding invoices for payment and placing orders with suppliers

I have gained considerable experience working with a variety of performers and venues.

December 2006 – July 2009: The Royal Theatre, Westley. Part-time box office assistant.

During my time at university I worked at the theatre on a part-time basis. I was responsible for selling and issuing tickets to customers and dealing with their enquiries.

SKILLS

Organisational abilities
I enjoy juggling different tasks and as the company I work for usually runs two or three shows at any one time, I have come up with effective systems for keeping track of each project, including progress charts and spreadsheets.

Communication skills
I am confident dealing with a range of people, including contractors, performers, suppliers and members of the public. During my current role I have been responsible for ensuring that all members of the team are kept up to date with schedule changes.

Rosie Jones 2010 (rosiejones@example.com)

Negotiation skills

All the costs associated with our productions have to stay on budget. In my current role, I have been responsible for ordering brochures, tickets and printed flyers. This has involved negotiating with local printers to bring these items in on budget. I am pleased to say that I have managed to save the company approximately 7% of their printing budget this year, by continued negotiations.

EDUCATION AND QUALIFICATIONS

September 2006 to June 2009, Westley University
BA (Hons) Business studies 2:2

During my degree I took the following modules:

- principles of marketing
- principles of organisation and management
- business information systems
- business economics
- marketing strategy and management
- international business
- human resource management
- operations management
- marketing of services
- advanced corporate finance
- business planning.

September 1999 to June 2006, St Theresa's Comprehensive School, Eastborough
A levels in:

- business studies (A)
- English literature (C)
- information and communication technology (D).

8 GCSEs at grades A*-C (including English, maths and science).

INTERESTS

I enjoy the arts and like to see live music as often as I can. I also play the violin for the Eastborough String Orchestra. I have recently taken part in a concert in aid of a local hospice; I helped to promote the concert and took responsibility for writing and printing the programme.

REFERENCES

Available on request.

The next functional CV belongs to Keisha who is sending her CV out on spec to local hairdressing salons, as she is looking for a junior position with training. Keisha highlights the skills she has that she feels are relevant for hairdressing. She also gives examples of when she has demonstrated these skills and qualities.

Keisha Stone

23a Marlton Rise
London
SW22 7DF
Mobile number: 07771111111
Email: keishas@anymail.com

I am hardworking and would like to train as a hairdresser. I am very creative and I enjoy putting together different looks for my friends. I work well with other people and would like to be part of a team in a salon.

Work experience

July 2009 – current: Colours Nail Salon. Part-time receptionist.
My duties include:

- keeping the salon tidy and wiping down surfaces

- taking payments by cash, credit and debit cards

- selling gift vouchers, nail polishes and accessories.

October 2008: Perfect Styles
I worked at Perfect Styles (a local hairdressers) during my work experience placement in Year 11. I really enjoyed speaking to all the stylists and getting a better understanding of what the work involves.

Skills

Communication skills

- In my current position I take messages from suppliers and deal with enquiries from customers on the phone and in person.

- I also greet customers politely and efficiently, and keep the technicians informed about their appointments.

Teamwork skills

- Sometimes the technicians in the salon where I work ask me to help them display stock items or place deliveries with the suppliers – I am always happy to help.

- As the technicians where I work are always busy, I offer to help out, by cleaning up or refilling their supplies, whenever I can.

Creative skills

- I am part of a local youth group and helped out with the costumes, hair and makeup in a fashion show we put on. The show was inspired by Romeo and Juliet. I really enjoyed designing a sequined eye mask for one of the models, which I then made myself.

- I styled the hair of the models who took part in the fashion show we put on. I used tongs to curl the models' hair which I then pinned up loosely with tiny pearl grips.

- I read a lot of fashion magazines and enjoy creating various celebrities' hairstyles on my friends.

Education

2004 – 2009 Marlton School

GCSEs:
- Art (grade B)

- Drama (grade B)

- English (grade C)

- Maths (grade E)

- Applied science (grade DD)

Interests

I enjoy dancing and I regularly attend a street dance class to learn new routines and techniques. I also like socialising with friends from my youth group and organising fundraising events and activities.

References

Mrs Latitia Bennett
Manager
Colours Nail Salon
27 Kenham High Street
London
SW22 1XB

020 8147 9789

Mr Yasser Khan
Youth Group Leader
The Lookout Youth Group
c/o Kenham Community Centre
389 Fletchley Road
London
SW22 8HR

020 8877 3232

The final functional CV belongs to Kevin who is applying for a job as a labourer. The job advert Kevin is responding to asks for someone reliable with practical skills. Although he sat five GCSEs he only passed three, so Kevin has decided to only list these. As Kevin does not have many qualifications he has made his skills, abilities and work experience the main focus of his CV.

CURRICULUM VITAE
Kevin Jameson
11 Stone House Court, Newborough NB1 5SD
Tel: 01888 555555; Mobile: 07879 222222; Email: kevinJ@example.co.uk

PERSONAL PROFILE

I am a hardworking, reliable person and enjoy practical work. I like working as part of a team and always try my best to get a job done. I would like to learn new skills and am prepared to work hard.

SKILLS AND ABILITIES

- Excellent practical skills. I have spent the summer helping my uncle renovate his house; I can use a cement mixer and helped clear an old site and lay foundations for a new shed.

- Driving licence. I recently passed my driving test and have my own car.

- Teamworking skills. I am a member of a local football team and enjoy working with other people.

WORK EXPERIENCE

August 2008 – present: Tony's Building Supplies, Newborough. Assistant.
I help to unload deliveries, put stock away, and pick items for customers' orders. I also update the stock database.

EDUCATION

September 2003 – June 2008: Newborough Comprehensive School.
ASDAN level 2 certificate in personal effectiveness
GCSEs in: design and technology – product design (C), maths (D), drama (E).

Chapter eight

Completing application forms

"But it clearly said 'Continue on a separate sheet if necessary'..."

This chapter:

- gives you general tips on filling in application forms and how to tackle the different sections

- looks at specific things you'll need to consider when completing either paper or online forms

- provides advice on completing applications for different types of opportunities – to apply for jobs, Apprenticeships, college courses and university places.

Why application forms?

Application forms are used for a number of purposes. You will normally have to complete one to apply for:

- vacancies for part-time or temporary jobs or full-time positions (unless a CV is acceptable)
- Apprenticeships
- college courses
- university courses.

You may also have to fill in applications for other purposes, such as for work experience placements or voluntary opportunities.

It might seem tedious to have to fill in an application form when you could submit a CV, but they do have advantages.

- The format is prepared for you. You just fill in the blank spaces; the amount of space provided suggests how much you should write.
- The form will tell you what information you have to provide and in what order, so you don't have to make decisions about these.
- Standardised forms help organisations treat applicants fairly and equally – it's easier to make direct comparisons between applicants and forms ensure the organisation gets all the information it needs.

On the downside, compared with CVs, forms can give you less flexibility to express yourself. As each application form is different, they can take quite a bit of time to complete. Also, some organisations use the same form for all opportunities, so it can prove difficult to find an appropriate space to give the information you want to get across.

Later in this chapter, there's information on some of the specific things you need to know when it comes to completing applications for the opportunities listed above, and for completing online and paper forms. Firstly, although forms vary widely, there are some general tips on completing most applications.

The main sections

Personal information

You'll be asked to give your **name** and **address** – don't forget your postcode.

You'll also be asked for **telephone numbers**. It's probably best to cover all bases by giving your home, mobile and work number (if you're already in a job and it's appropriate to receive calls). If you give your home number, make sure members of your family know so they will be prepared if they take calls for you.

If an **email** address is requested, make sure this is a sensible one – see page 53.

Some application forms ask for your **date of birth, age, marital status, nationality, ethnic origin** etc, although these may be included in a separate equal opportunities monitoring form (see later in this chapter).

Most forms will ask whether you are **eligible to work or study in the UK**; at some stage of the application process you may have to provide proof of your status and entitlement to remain and/or work or study in the UK.

Education, training and qualifications

You will normally be asked to state what **schools, colleges, universities** etc you have attended. Unless asked otherwise, don't put the full addresses of institutions, just their names and the towns/cities where they are based. Don't give the details of schools you attended before the age of 11.

When asked to list your **qualifications**, you may be given boxes for all the relevant information. If not, state the:

- type of qualification, level and subject
- grades you achieved
- month and year they were gained.

Mention any specific modules, units or projects that are particularly relevant for the opportunity you are applying for.

Present your information in a consistent and easy-to-read format. For example, avoid mixing date styles – stick to either August 2011 or 8/11.

If your grades are poor, or you don't have any qualifications, refer to the advice on page 40. If any of your qualifications are unusual or were gained abroad, you could add a note comparing them with more commonly known ones. You can always address these kinds of issues in a covering letter or email – see Chapter nine.

If you haven't finished a course yet, list what you are doing and when you will get the results. If requested, or if you think it will help your application, give your predicted grades.

In this section don't forget to include details of any relevant **training courses** you may have done through work, or other **short courses, distance-learning** programmes or **evening classes**.

Employment history

This section mainly relates to job applications. If you're **currently in employment**, you'll be asked to give details of:

- your employer (name, contact details etc)
- your job title
- the month and year that you started
- your main duties and responsibilities. Include anything that you consider to be of particular relevance to the opportunity you're applying for.

In a similar way, you will also have to provide details of any **previous employment**. Always start with your most recent job and work backwards. Don't forget to include any part-time, temporary or voluntary jobs, work experience etc; make it clear what type of employment each was. Include all the details bulleted above, although it may not be necessary to give as much detail about your duties and responsibilities – you need to judge what information is relevant for the opportunity you are applying for.

You may be asked to note your **current salary** or pay per hour. If you are asked for your **expected salary**, be realistic about what this might be, but don't undersell yourself either!

You may also be asked your **reasons for leaving previous jobs**. If you're a school or college leaver, make it clear that any jobs you've had have been temporary or part-time positions. If you've moved on from a job because you wanted to widen your skills and experience, return to education or go for promotion, these things will be viewed in a positive light. Selectors will normally understand if you've been made redundant. If you've been dismissed from a job, you need to be honest. However, you should try to explain the circumstances, perhaps in a covering letter/email or in the supporting information section (see below). Say what you've learned from the experience, what you would do differently next time etc. Whatever you do, don't blame someone else – you may be viewed as a troublemaker or the selectors may even know people in that organisation!

Competency-based questions

Increasingly, selectors are using competency-based questions where you are asked to give examples of occasions when you have used particular skills. These questions are usually used instead of providing you with a section where you give supporting information (see below). The benefit of competency-based questions is that it's clear what the selectors are looking for. There's advice on how to tackle such questions in Chapter four.

Supporting information

In most standard forms, there's usually a section that tells you to give additional information in support of your application or asks you to say why you are interested in the opportunity. It's usually a big, empty box, but it's an important part of your application!

Before you launch into this section, it's a good idea to set the scene by stating **why you want the opportunity**. This is your chance to show how motivated you are! Obviously you shouldn't say that it's on your bus route or because you've heard that the pay is good. Selectors want to make sure that you've given some serious thought to your reasons for applying. They want to find out **why** you want the particular opportunity and **why** with them. After all, if you 'fit' the opportunity and organisation, you are more likely to enjoy what you are doing and work to your full potential. Always be positive – don't say that you don't like what you're doing at the moment.

Examples of responses include:

> *'I'm interested in working for your organisation because it has a good reputation for staff development and excellent customer service.'*
>
> *'I'm particularly interested in this opportunity because it would allow me to use my existing skills and to develop further.'*

Refer back to Chapter three to help you decide what's important to you.

It's a good idea to use the principles of competencies to help you structure the rest of your supporting information section. Your aim is to demonstrate to selectors how your particular skills, aptitudes, experience and knowledge match what they are looking for, i.e. that you have what it takes! It's also a chance to show that you've done your research on the organisation and the opportunity.

Chapter two will help you identify what criteria selectors are looking for. For each of the main selection criteria (preferably in the same order as they have been given to you), use the competency approach to show that you are a suitable candidate for the opportunity. Refer to Chapter four for examples of how to tackle competency-based questions. As a reminder, if one of the criteria is that you are able to work in a team, draw on something from your experience, such as when you successfully worked on a group project. Using the CAR approach, set the scene (context), describe what you did (action) and explain what happened (result). It's important to give specific examples with full descriptions.

If you're applying for a job, ideally the examples should be drawn from a range of experiences at work. However, if you are applying for your first full-time job, a training opportunity or course, you can draw on the transferable skills that you have gained through your school or college studies, volunteering, work experience, interests, hobbies etc, as well as any paid work you have undertaken.

Always write about yourself using 'positive' words and try to identify things that make you stand out from the crowd. Chapter three shows how you can gather lots of information about yourself, which you can use in this section of the application.

Other typical questions

As application forms vary, other questions you may be asked include those listed below.

- **Why have you chosen to apply here?** Find out as much as you can about the employer or college/university. You could mention things like their facilities, reputation, culture, goals, market position, clients, range of products or services, commitment to staff development and so on.

- **What has been your greatest achievement to date?** Your response will show what you believe is important and what you consider to be success. You should explain why you think your example is so important to you, what it has taught you and how you have used this experience. Don't feel you have to come up with something amazing, such as being the youngest person to scale Everest! Things like leading a school project, gaining a badge at Scouts or Guides, winning an award for art, getting a prize for sport, or being involved in volunteering are all good examples of achievements.

- **What extracurricular activities and interests do you have?** This can not only indicate that you are a well-balanced person, but that you are able to juggle commitments, can work with a range of people, have had the chance to broaden your skills etc. Make sure you stress what you have gained from your activities and interests and how these might be of value for the opportunity. Mention any special achievements or positions of responsibility held. Don't include anything you wouldn't be happy to talk about should you be invited for an interview.

- **What are your strengths and weaknesses?** Don't give one-word answers – give examples of where your strengths have been used etc. Although we all have weaknesses, try to present these as areas for development. It's a good idea to focus on things that you are aware of and have already taken action to improve. So, if you are the kind of person who pays attention to detail, perhaps you could say that you've had to work on seeing the bigger picture. If you're full of ideas at the start of a project, perhaps you could say that you've had to work on staying focused in order to complete it.

References

You are normally asked to provide the details of two people who may be approached for a reference. If you are employed, one referee should be your current manager or supervisor. If you are a school or college leaver, you can usually give details of a headteacher, tutor or lecturer. A suitable second referee may be a previous employer or leader of a voluntary or youth organisation that you have been involved with. Both referees should be in positions of some responsibility and be able to comment on your ability to do the job or course. Relatives and friends are not acceptable referees.

You usually have to indicate whether you are happy for your referees to be contacted – either before or after an interview. Make sure that you ask your referees' permission before giving out their names and contact details!

Equal opportunities monitoring and disclosures

Many application forms have an equal opportunities section – this may be on a separate form (paper or online) or on a sheet that can be torn off the main application. Although you don't have to complete it, organisations use this information to check whether they are unintentionally discriminating against any groups of people in their advertising etc. The information isn't used in the selection process.

You are likely to be asked for details such as your age, gender, sexual orientation, race, ethnicity, nationality, religion, beliefs and marital status. You will also be asked for details of any disability and perhaps whether you will require specific arrangements to be made so that you can attend an interview.

If you are asked about any criminal records, make sure you are honest. If you are applying for certain opportunities, such as to work with children, you will have to undergo criminal record checks before being offered a position. Don't forget that you can explain your circumstances in a covering letter or email (see Chapter nine). Some criminal convictions and cautions become 'spent' after a period of time, which means that for certain opportunities they don't have to be declared. If necessary, get advice, for example from an organisation like NACRO: www.nacro.org.

Declaration

The information you give in your application may be checked, especially if you get the job or college/training place, so always tell the truth. There's usually a section at the end of the form that asks you to declare that the information is true and complete. If you leave out important information or tell lies, this may be found out later down the line and could lead to rejection, dismissal or expulsion.

General tips

Sloppily completed application forms give the impression that you don't really want the opportunity you are applying for. They also indicate that you are the type of person who doesn't pay attention to details. Completing a form is also your opportunity to demonstrate your writing skills – this is important for many jobs and courses.

The person looking at your form may have hundreds to go through, so make it as easy as possible for the selectors to read and understand. Here are some general tips for all types of applications.

- If possible, read the form carefully all the way through before you start.

- If you are provided with instructions or guidance notes, follow them precisely.

- If any section of the form doesn't apply to you put N/A (i.e. not applicable) – this shows that you haven't missed out a section in error.

- Make sure that all your answers are concise and relevant. Don't waffle.

- Take care with abbreviations, jargon etc – only use them if you are sure they will be understood, otherwise explain what they mean.

- Make sure that all the information is accurate. Common errors include putting today's date rather than your date of birth and misspelling the name of the organisation or course you are applying to!

- Be as consistent as possible in the way your information (e.g. qualifications) is presented.

- Organisations are increasingly using electronic scanning techniques to find the key words that describe the skills etc they are looking for. Find out which skills etc are expected and make sure you mention these appropriately – but don't overdo it! Although scanning lends itself to online applications, be aware that paper applications can be scanned and the same word-search techniques applied.

- Keep your writing fairly formal and use short, easy-to-understand sentences and familiar words. Consider breaking up big blocks of text by using paragraphs, headings and bullets.

- Leave the form after the first draft so that you have an opportunity to rethink what you've written. Then keep working on it until you're completely happy that it gets across exactly the message you want.

- Check that you haven't missed out any questions and that you have addressed all of its parts – some questions include two or three sub-questions.

- Check and double-check your spelling, punctuation and grammar. Don't rely on a spellchecker as it won't pick up on everything. Stick to British spellings rather than US, e.g. use 'organise' instead of 'organize' and 'colour' not 'color'.

- Complete and attach any accompanying documents, such as an equal opportunities monitoring form. Unless you are specifically asked to do so, don't attach or email a CV.

- Write a brief covering letter or email (see Chapter nine).

- When you think you have finished, ask someone you trust to read your application through and provide you with feedback.

- Keep a copy for future reference – you may need to refer to it before an interview. You could also use it as a starting point when applying for other opportunities.

Paper forms

If you're working on a paper form, practise on a photocopy or spare sheet of paper until you're sure that you've got everything correct.

Write as legibly as possible. Look out for instructions, such as to use black pen or to write in block capitals, and make sure you follow them. Unless told otherwise, use black pen so that the form can easily be photocopied or scanned. Try not to write too big or too small. Avoid crossing things out or using correction fluid/tape unless you really have to. If you do make an error, try to get another copy of the form or strike through the error as neatly as possible.

The size of the boxes on the form will indicate roughly how much you should write. If there's not enough space, you may be allowed to continue on a separate sheet, but check whether or not this is acceptable. If you do, put your name at the top of each sheet and include brief details of the opportunity you are applying for, e.g. the job or course title and reference.

When you've finished, choose a sensible-looking envelope – usually white or brown. Avoid folding the form too many times – it might be preferable to use an A4 envelope. Be careful when writing the address.

Include the person's name and their department if you can as this can speed up delivery in a large organisation. Always include the postcode.

Post your application in good time to meet the closing date. Make sure that you use the correct postage. If you are at all close to the deadline, it's worth paying extra for next-day delivery. If you can, deliver the application by hand.

Online forms

Although applications are increasingly completed online, if you're unable to access the internet, or have difficulties, seek advice from the employer or training provider. It may well be that paper forms can be used in these circumstances.

When completing an online form, give it as much attention as you would if you were filling it in by hand. Be particularly careful with your spelling as you may not be able to use a spellchecker.

There are various types of online forms, but to simplify things, let's consider two main types:

- **forms that you can download**, complete and submit online; these tend to follow a similar format to paper forms and you can read the whole form in advance

- **forms that cannot be downloaded** – they are designed specifically for electronic delivery and help to speed up the application process. Some forms are **interactive**, so you will be presented with different questions depending on your answers to earlier ones. With non-downloadable forms, you can't usually read the whole form in advance.

Downloadable forms

Try to work on a copy first. If you print it off, you could complete this by hand. If you work on the computer, make sure that you save the form each time you work on it.

Once you're happy with the application, find out how the organisation would like it submitted. As you can't write on extra sheets of paper, you could include any supplementary information in an email. For advice on writing a covering email, see Chapter nine. If you have more than one version of the form saved on your computer, make sure that you send off the correct one!

Non-downloadable forms

These applications can be tricky as you might not be able to backtrack to change or check things you've already put, and you may have to complete them in one sitting. Some online forms are timed – if so, you are given a fixed period to complete each section and any online tests.

Here are some tips:

- consider finding out what to expect when completing the application – you could contact the organisation or ask previous applicants, perhaps through a relevant forum or blog

- make sure that you are fully familiar with the requirements for the opportunity, that you have done some research on the organisation and that you have gathered together all the personal information you are likely to need – your CV if you have one, certificates etc

- if the application includes some tests, be prepared for these – see Chapter ten

- set yourself enough time to work through the form without interruptions

- find out whether it's possible to paste in some of the more lengthy information from a wordprocessing program

- there are sometimes word limits, so you need to be concise

- if there are 'next' buttons, take care not to click on these until you're happy with what you've written; similarly, don't press the submit button before you are completely happy with your whole application

- if you can't keep a copy, jot down or take a screen shot of anything that you may not recall at a later date.

Applications for different opportunities

Job applications

Many employers ask you to fill in an application form instead of sending in a CV. Although lots of employers now expect you to apply online, some still issue paper forms.

You may find yourself having to complete more than one form. For instance, if you apply online for a job with a major employer, there may be some initial questions to answer about your expectations, experience and skills. These are sometimes used to filter out unsuitable applicants at an early stage. Alternatively, you may be applying for a job through a recruitment agency or an online job site. They will want to know quite a bit about you so that they can put you forward for suitable jobs. You would then need to fill in further applications for specific vacancies when they arise.

Apprenticeship applications

Government-funded Apprenticeships are available in around 80 broad areas of work – from accounting to veterinary nursing. They allow you to work, train, earn money and gain nationally-recognised qualifications. Most involve some study at a college or training centre, possibly on day- or block-release from work.

In **England**, there are **Apprenticeships** and **Advanced Apprenticeships** leading to qualifications at levels 2 and 3 respectively. For information, visit: www.apprenticeships.org.uk.

In **Wales, Foundation Apprenticeships** lead to level 2 qualifications and **Apprenticeships** to level 3. For information, see: www.careerswales.com/16to19 (click on 'Work and training' and then 'Apprenticeships/training').

How to apply

Many young people apply for Apprenticeships during their final year at school, with a view to starting in the summer months, especially if the training is linked to a college course that begins in September. However, you can start most programmes at any time.

To apply for an Apprenticeship there are a number of different starting points, or combinations of these. For instance you can:

- contact your local Connexions/careers service for information on local opportunities

- apply through an appropriate Apprenticeship provider – these are organisations that manage Apprenticeships; they may be further education colleges, private training providers or large employers

- apply directly to an employer offering an Apprenticeship opportunity

- visit the appropriate Apprenticeship website (see above) – there's lots of information and online vacancy matching services where you can register, search for vacancies and apply online. This is becoming the most common starting point.

Bear in mind that you may have to complete more than one application form, for example:

- if you apply through one of the Apprenticeship websites (see above), you complete an online form

- if you apply through a training provider, there may be a form to complete

- when you find a potential employer, they may expect you to fill in another application

- there may be yet another form to complete when you apply for a college course as part of your Apprenticeship programme!

During the Apprenticeship application process, you're sometimes expected to take tests (see Chapter ten for more information).

General tips

While Apprenticeship application forms vary, make sure you read the vacancy carefully and target your application accordingly – think carefully about the skills and experience the employer or training provider is looking for.

Apart from all the usual questions about you and your qualifications, you are likely to be asked your reasons for choosing to do a particular Apprenticeship. This is your chance to present yourself effectively and persuade an employer or training provider to shortlist you for the next stage of the recruitment process. You need to show that you've really thought about what you want to do and researched the content of the Apprenticeship programme and the employer or training organisation you're applying to. So, don't write something too simplistic like, 'I want to be a beautician' or 'I'd like to be a builder'.

Mention any courses you have already taken that relate to the Apprenticeship you want to do. For example, you may have done a GCSE in applied business, which would be helpful for an Apprenticeship in business and administration.

Ensure that you emphasise your relevant experience and transferable skills (see Chapter three) and give examples of situations when you have used them, e.g. through your work experience, school or college work, part-time jobs, volunteering, hobbies, interests etc.

In addition to employers and training providers wanting to check that you have the skills and ability to do the job, they also want to ensure that you have the necessary interest and commitment to do all the training and courses required. This might involve part-time attendance at college and doing coursework in your spare time. Give examples that show you can motivate yourself and manage your time effectively. Make sure that you convey your enthusiasm for the work and training involved. You could mention any long-term career goals.

Below is an example of one person's Apprenticeship application.

'I am interested in an Advanced Apprenticeship in children's care, learning and development, as I would like to work in a nursery. I have considerable experience of working with children – I have a young brother who I look after a lot, and I regularly babysit for my neighbours' children. In addition, I did two weeks' work experience at Happy Days Nursery. The nursery manager has provided me with a reference.

I enjoy working with children and relate to them well. I am patient and caring with a lot of energy. I believe that I have a good understanding of the needs of children and enjoy helping them to develop. I work well in a team; during my work experience I was involved in 'healthy-eating week' and organised a colourful display on the subject. In order to develop my confidence when speaking with parents, I've taken advice from the experienced nursery staff.

Last year I completed seven GCSEs. As you will see, one of these was home economics: child development, for which I got an A*.

The Apprenticeship will give me the opportunity to gain real work experience and to achieve recognised qualifications – both of which are important to me.'

Before sending off or submitting your form, check your spelling, punctuation and grammar and ask someone you trust to read it through.

Applying through an Apprenticeship website

Once you've registered on the relevant website (see above), it's important to keep your password and user name safe. The application process is very straightforward as you are guided through each step. Take as much care as you would with any paper application. You can save the form and create a draft copy and you can also preview your application and check it over before you send it.

You can reuse the information from one vacancy to help you apply for another, as much of it will still be relevant. However, remember that it's important to tailor your application to the vacancy you're applying for. Once you've applied, you can track the progress of your application online.

College course applications

Once you have decided which course you want to do and where, you will need to complete an application. You can usually do this online. Alternatively, there may be a separate form available from the college, a pull-out sheet in the prospectus or you could print out a form from their website. In England, the Government is working towards a Common Application Process. This means that, in the future, you will only have to apply for courses and training (including Apprenticeships) through one process, rather than having to complete different applications for different opportunities.

Apart from all the usual information required, you may be asked to state briefly your reasons for applying for the course of your choice. Try to mention:

- what interests you about the subject
- how it fits in with your long-term career goals
- why you have chosen the particular college – it might have excellent facilities for your subject or have a good reputation for the course you want to do
- your relevant experience and skills.

If you are unsure how to answer any of the questions, speak to someone at the college; staff in student services can usually help. If you are still at school, you could also ask for advice from your careers coordinator, tutor or teacher.

Once you have completed your application, make sure that you submit it in good time – popular courses fill up very quickly and there may be limited places.

University applications

Applying through UCAS

Applications for most full-time higher education courses, i.e. those leading to foundation degrees, HNDs, degrees etc, are through UCAS.

You will make your application through 'Apply' – a secure, web-based system accessed through registering on: www.ucas.com.

Your teachers, tutor or personal/careers adviser can show you how to register. They can also help you complete your application. Apply includes a help guide and you can save your progress as you go.

Aim to give yourself as much time as possible to choose courses (you are allowed up to five choices) and to complete your application. There are certain dates by which your application should reach UCAS, so find out which date applies to you.

Writing your personal statement

Not many applicants are invited to interview – most are selected on their qualification results or predicted results and application. This means that you have to convince admissions tutors that you are the right person for the course and selectors often rely heavily on what you say in your personal statement when making decisions.

Apply allows you to write up to 4,000 characters (including spaces), so you have to be clear and concise. Your statement can be wordprocessed and then copied and pasted into Apply.

Have a look at Entry Profiles on the UCAS website (found under 'Course Search'). Entry Profiles give details about the course, the personal qualities or experience required etc – try to address these in your statement. It's up to you what you say in your personal statement, but the kinds of things you should include are listed below.

- Mention any **future plans or career aspirations**. This will show that you've given some thought to your course choice and it demonstrates your commitment.

- Explain what aspects of your **current or previous course/s** you enjoy and what you're keen to learn more about in the future. You could also mention particular skills you have developed during your studies or training so far, such as time management and teamwork.

- Describe **why you have chosen the course/s** you have listed. Say what particularly interests you about the subject/s. Try to convey some understanding and enthusiasm. You could mention any journals, books etc you have read and show you are aware of current issues in your chosen field. Say if you have talked to people who study or work in the area you are interested in. This shows you have taken the time to research your career options, can develop your knowledge and give you realistic expectations; perhaps this person will even be able to give you support in the future.

- Especially if relevant to your chosen subject, describe any **work experience, paid job** or **voluntary work** you have done. Mention any transferable skills you have developed, e.g. communication skills or problem solving.

- Give details of skills and achievements you have gained through **activities** such as Young Enterprise, the Duke of Edinburgh's Award or volunteer programmes.

- Describe your **hobbies and social, sport or leisure interests**, including any positions of responsibility held, skills developed, things you are particularly proud of etc. If you have lots of interests, focus on the most relevant two or three.

In addition to the things described above, you could mention any **sponsorships or placements** you have secured or that you have applied for. If you're planning on deferring your entry because of a **gap year**, state what you intend to do during this time. If you've been involved in any **widening participation schemes**, such as summer schools, describe your involvement in these. If relevant, explain any circumstances that have led to **poorer than expected results** or predicted grades.

Don't expect to finish your personal statement in one sitting! Start by planning an outline of what you want to include and then write a number of drafts. At some stage, it's a good idea to leave it for a while so that you can mull it over. Once you feel it's pretty much there, ask at least one other person you trust (such as teacher) to read it through and comment.

Don't be tempted to copy a personal statement from someone else or from a website. UCAS operates similarity detection tests and will notify you and your chosen universities if there's a significant similarity between your statement and any others.

Before finalising your personal statement, here's a checklist of questions you should ask yourself.

- Have I included everything and expanded on the most important points?

- Is the statement written in a logical order?

- Have I used paragraphs (and, possibly, headings) to break up the text? Have I varied the start of each paragraph, avoiding beginning each with 'I'?

- Is the overall tone positive and enthusiastic? You should never put yourself or your skills down! See Chapter three for a list of positive words you can use to describe yourself.

- Have I checked my grammar, spelling and punctuation? The personal statement is also evidence of your writing skills and ability to pay attention to detail!

- Has someone checked over my personal statement?

- Have I saved or printed out a copy?

What happens next?

You can check on the progress of your application using the online UCAS Track system. When universities have made their decision, you will normally be notified through Track. If you have not yet taken your exams, offers are usually conditional on you gaining certain grades. You don't usually need to reply to offers until you have received all your decisions. You can only hold up to two offers. You must notify UCAS, by the date shown on Track, which offer you wish to firmly accept and which you want to accept as an insurance place.

If you don't receive any offers or you have decided not to accept any, Extra allows you to apply for a place before Clearing begins in August.

Find out more

For more information on Apply, writing personal statements, Track, Extra, Clearing etc, see: www.ucas.com.

There are a number of books to help you apply to university, including:

How to Complete Your UCAS Application and *How to Write a Winning UCAS Personal Statement* – both published by Trotman, part of Crimson Publishing, £12.99 each.

Applying to University: The Essential Guide – published by Need2Know, £8.99.

Finally

Remember that when completing application forms for any opportunity, whilst you need to be honest, don't be afraid to sell yourself – be proud of your achievements!

Chapter nine

Covering letters and emails

"Good cv, but it is let down by the covering letter."

This chapter includes:

- advice on writing a covering letter
- practical tips on how to get your documents to an employer
- examples of covering letters.

You've slaved over your CV or application form and now all you need to do is submit it. This might sound pretty straightforward but you should approach this task with the same amount of care and attention as you put into your CV or application form. As with your CV, you should tailor your covering letter to the job you are applying for.

You can choose to post a printed hard copy of your documents or email them to the employer. Whatever your decision most of the advice in this chapter will apply to you. If you are emailing your CV/application form to an employer, the email will act as your covering letter.

What's the point of a covering letter?

Whether you are sending your CV on spec to employers, or you're sending a CV or an application form to apply for a vacancy, it's important to attach a covering letter that will introduce you to the employer in a positive way. Your CV or application form will give the employer all the details they need about your qualifications, experience and skills, but your covering letter is another chance to really sell yourself and highlight why you're right for the role. Obviously, you need to keep your letter brief, so the trick is to only mention your key 'selling points' – the **strongest** reasons why you are suited to the role, rather than all the reasons.

Your covering letter is the first chance you will get to impress employers. Ideally it should:

- be brief – your letter should fit onto one side of A4

- be well thought out – don't waffle or repeat all the information from the CV or application form that you've attached

- be positive and demonstrate your enthusiasm for the role

- show that you have done your research and know a bit about the company or organisation.

You can use your covering letter to show that you've used your initiative and done some research about the company. Before you write your letter, find out a bit more about the company – what do they do, what successes have they had, who are their customers/users? Try to use this information in your letter. Most companies have websites that will include this type of information.

You may not have had the space to mention something important in your CV or application form, in which case your covering letter can also give you the opportunity to tell the employer about any other points that are relevant to your application.

Your covering letter is also the place to explain anything unusual or negative on your CV/application form. Perhaps there are gaps in your employment history, you got poor grades in your exams or you're looking for a complete change of career; whatever the issue, you can explain it in your covering letter.

Content – what your letter needs to include

If you're sending a CV on spec, your letter needs to include the following information:

- your contact details

- the type of work you are looking for

- what you have to offer the employer (your most relevant skills, qualifications and/or experience)

- when you are available to meet the employer.

If you're sending a CV or application form to an employer to apply for a vacancy you've seen advertised, your letter needs to include the following information:

- the title and reference number of the job you are applying for, and where you saw the advert

- your contact details

- brief details of why you are right for the job (your most relevant skills, qualifications and/or experience)

- the reasons why you want the job.

Your covering letter needs to be a short, impressive introduction to your application that makes the employer want to look at your CV/application form. A good way of structuring your letter is shown below.

- Paragraph 1 – a brief introduction to yourself including the details of the job you are applying for, or your 'career objective' (if applying on spec). Give details of why you want this particular job, with this particular organisation. Sound enthusiastic and show you've done your research.

- Paragraph 2 – highlight your education, skills, competencies and any other information you think they should know. Remember to target everything you write to the vacancy you are applying for or the job that you are interested in (if you're applying on spec).

- Paragraph 3 – positive final comments, then give your availability for interview, or say that you would like an opportunity to visit them if your letter is being written speculatively.

Some job adverts give specific instructions for covering letters, such as 'please include details of your salary expectations'; in this situation, follow the instructions and be sure to include the information that you've been asked for.

Who to send your letter or email to

Whether you are writing in response to a particular job advert, or on spec, you must get your letter or email to the correct person. Who to address and send your letter/email to might be obvious if the name was stated in the job advert or was with the information sent to you by the organisation. However, if you aren't sure, (this may well be the case if you are sending your CV on spec) it's worth taking the time and effort to find out who the correct person is. Check on the employer's website or give them a call and ask. It's a small but important point, because it shows the reader that you are able to use your initiative. Also, unless you address the letter/email to the correct person there's a chance it may get lost. You simply have to phone the organisation and ask the switchboard who would be the most appropriate person.

Remember, if you are addressing your letter/email to a named person, you should sign off with 'Yours sincerely'. However, if you really can't find the correct person to address your letter to and you need to start with 'Dear Sir' or 'Dear Madam', you should end with 'Yours faithfully'.

How to get your letter to the employer

You have a choice of how to get your documents to the employer. The most popular and easiest ways of doing this are by sending hard copies in the post or by attaching your documents to an email. You could also choose to deliver your letter by hand – this can be a great way of making contact with the employer and creating a good impression early on. Generally speaking, how you submit your documents is up to you; however there are circumstances when one method is preferable to another.

If you are responding to a job advert, you should follow the instructions in the advert when submitting your CV or application form e.g. don't post a hard copy if the employer has asked applicants to email their details in.

If you are sending a CV to an employer on spec, it's usually best to send it via email. Most companies work electronically now and it's much easier for them to store your details, or forward your CV on to the correct department, if they have an electronic copy. However, if you're unsure, you could call the company's human resources department and ask them how they prefer to receive CVs.

Posting your documents

If you decide to post hard copies of your documents, your covering letter should be wordprocessed so that it looks professional. Use a clear, easy-to-read font such as Arial, Verdana or Times New Roman in point size 10 or 12. Leaving a space between paragraphs is also a good idea.

Some employers ask applicants to submit a handwritten covering letter. This is quite rare and would usually only happen if the job required an applicant with clear, presentable handwriting. If you are asked to do this, use good quality, plain white or cream paper – don't use lined paper with holes punched down the side. You should use a blue or black pen that writes nicely and doesn't leave ink splodges on the page!

Tips!

- Print your covering letter on good quality white, or cream paper.

- Sign the covering letter with a blue or black pen, but print your name below the signature so that it can be read easily.

- Don't fold your documents too many times – use a plain white or brown A4 envelope if possible.

- If you are posting your CV and it is more than one page long, print each page on a separate piece of paper and staple the pages together (or make sure your name is on each sheet).

- Post your documents first class, and check you've attached enough stamps.

Emailing your documents

Most of us use email or electronic communication every day, so it's easy to slip into the usual habits when you're emailing a potential employer. But the email that accompanies your CV or application form needs to be as professional as your other documents. Treat the email as a covering letter and follow the advice above – **never** use text speak, internet slang or chatspeak!

Tips!

- Make the subject of the email very clear, such as 'application for vacancy' and the job title or reference number of the vacancy you are interested in.

- All attachments (including your CV) need to be clearly labelled; ideally the filename should include your name and the reference or name of the job you are applying for e.g. MBrown186administrator

- It's a good idea to set up the delivery or read receipt function on your account so you can be sure that your email has arrived.

- Make sure you have actually attached your CV or application form before you send the email – it's very easy to forget!

- Remember to check your inbox regularly for any replies!

Examples of covering letters

With the help of the advice given above, you shouldn't have any problems writing a covering letter. To give you an idea of how to set out your letter, have a look at the examples below. The first is a covering letter to be sent with a CV in response to a job advert. The second example is an email sent to an employer on spec. The last example is sent with a CV to apply for an Apprenticeship.

10 Gilbert Avenue
Anytown
Glos GL2 3BL
01222 343536

Mr J. Brown
Corfield Council
Anytown
Glos GL5 5PL

5 October 2010

Dear Mr Brown

Sports development administrative assistant, vacancy reference 4521

I would like to apply for the sports development administrative assistant vacancy advertised in the *Gazette*, on Friday 1st October. I am very interested in sports development work and would especially like to help Corfield Council develop its new *Cutting Truancy Through Sport* campaign.

Last year I completed a BTEC National Diploma in sport, which included a unit on sports development work. Since then, I have been working as a member of an administrative team at Redwood Pharmaceuticals. My duties have included scheduling meetings, filing, photocopying and updating the customer database. I am an organised and reliable worker. In my spare time, I am a member of a local netball team and have recently taken my Level 1 Award in Coaching Netball.

I would really like to move into an administrative position that relates to my interest in sports development work. I feel the skills that I have developed at Redwood Pharmaceuticals would be useful for this position. I have enclosed my CV and look forward to hearing from you. I am available for an interview at any time.

Yours sincerely

Karen Bluefield

Karen Bluefield

In the next covering letter, which was sent as an email, Jack is writing on spec to an employer, looking for work. Jack's email tells the employer about his strengths and the type of work he is looking for.

To: anne.reed@griggsltd.co.uk
Subject: Van driver available for work

19 King's Street
Redfearn
Lancashire RD3 3EE
01987 778865

Dear Ms Reed

I have just moved to the area and I am looking for work as a van driver. I am a reliable worker and have many qualities that I think would be of use to Griggs Ltd. I have attached my CV and I hope you will consider me for any driving vacancies you have in future.

I have 18 months' experience working for Jones Industries in London who would be willing to provide a reference for me. During that time I made deliveries both locally and within a 100-mile radius. I also:

- had an unbroken attendance record
- was always punctual
- was accident free
- had a good reputation with both Jones' staff and customers.

I am available for interview any day after the 11th October and hope to have an opportunity to speak to you in future.

Yours sincerely

Jack Simms

The next covering letter is sent by Darren, who is applying for an Apprenticeship in horticulture. The advert states that the employer is looking for someone with some experience of horticulture, who would be willing to work towards qualifications. Darren sends his letter, along with his CV, to the recruitment manager.

43 Barnaby Road,
Old Town
DW1 1JA

Friday 22nd October

Dear Mr Thompson,

Reference: horticulture apprenticeship vacancy

I am writing to apply for the horticulture apprenticeship with JD Morely Garden Services as advertised in the Old Town Chronicle.

I would like to apply as I am very interested in horticulture and enjoy working outside. I have just finished school and would like to continue learning in the workplace.

I have good practical skills and regularly help my uncle on his allotment. I help weed and prepare the soil for planting, by digging in compost and manure. I have recently learned how to prune fruit bushes and take cuttings, and enjoy learning new techniques. This experience has developed my interest in horticulture greatly, and helped me decide to aim for a career in this area.

I have enclosed my CV and look forward to hearing from you. I am available for interview at any time.

Yours sincerely

D. Hedges

Darren Hedges

Chapter ten

Tests and work samples

This chapter:

- describes the different types of tests that are used during the initial stages of selection

- will help you prepare to take tests

- explains how samples of work or set exercises can form part of the application process.

Selection tests

You may have to sit a test or a series of tests before you'll even be considered for an interview. In fact, tests are increasingly being used.

If you're expected to take a test at the same time as (or before) formally applying for an opportunity, you are likely to have to take it online at home. However, sometimes you are sent a test or task to do in the post and you have to send this in with your completed application form. Alternatively, you may be asked to go to a testing centre.

Who uses tests?

Tests are often used where there are lots of applications for a limited number of opportunities.

Tests are mainly used by **large employers** – such as certain Civil Service departments, the Armed Forces, fire and rescue services and some big companies. They help weed out unsuitable job applicants at an early stage of the application process. They can be used instead of specifying particular educational entry requirements, thereby opening up more opportunities for people to apply.

Some **Apprenticeship training providers** make use of tests, often as part of their online application processes. In this situation, tests can be used to:

- help decide what type of work would be particularly suitable for a candidate

- check that an applicant will be able to cope with the training and job requirements – this is particularly important for technical trades e.g. in the motor industry or construction sector

- decide at what level an applicant should enter training, i.e. level 2 or level 3.

For entry to some **college and university courses**, you may be asked to take an admissions test. The Entry Profiles on the UCAS website (through 'Course Search') should indicate whether you will be asked to sit a test.

The Universities of Oxford and Cambridge have their own tests for entry onto certain courses, such as maths, history and modern languages. Other admissions tests that may be used by universities include the: National Admissions Test for Law (LNAT); UK Clinical Aptitude Test (UKCAT) for entry to courses in medicine and dentistry and BioMedical Admissions Test (BMAT) for courses in medicine, veterinary science and biomedical science. These tests help universities to allocate places on courses that attract many highly qualified applicants. The tests are normally taken online at testing centres across the UK.

For more information on university admissions tests, see: www.ucas.com/students.

There are a number of publications that can help you prepare for specific university admissions tests, such as:

Passing the National Admissions Test for Law and *Passing the UKCAT and BMAT* – both published by Learning Matters, £15.00 each

How to Master the UKCAT and *How to Master the BMAT* – both published by Kogan Page, £14.99 each.

Types of tests

All kinds of tests can be used as part of the application process – sometimes they are generally referred to as 'psychometric tests'. Only certain tests lend themselves to the initial stages of application, so be aware that you may be expected to do other tests, such as group tasks, role plays or presentations, if you are invited to attend an interview or an assessment day.

Aptitude and ability tests

Aptitude tests can help selectors find out whether you have the potential to learn the skills and knowledge required for the job, training programme or course. **Ability tests** assess whether your skills and knowledge are good enough to start a job, training programme or course.

Most tests involve short answers or multiple-choice questions and give you a limited amount of time to complete them.

Examples of aptitude/ability tests include:

- **verbal tests** – you may be given a passage of text and then asked questions based on that information, or you may have to read and follow instructions or demonstrate your ability to spell and use correct grammar and punctuation

- **numerical tests** – these can involve basic arithmetical calculations (you may or may not be able to use a calculator) or you could be given a table, graph or set of statistics and asked to find the correct answers to a number of questions

- **abstract or spatial reasoning tests** – these assess your ability to apply logic – you may be given a sequence of shapes, numbers, diagrams etc and asked for the next one in the sequence.

If you are applying for a position with responsibility, such as a supervisory role, you may be asked to do an **e-tray test**. Within a set time you have to decide what you would do with items in an electronic in-box, e.g. delegate it, refer to someone else, deal with it immediately etc. Alternatively, you may be given a **situational judgement test**. This comprises short descriptions of job-related situations and for each you have to pick what you consider to be the most effective action. These kinds of tests aim to see how you might respond to challenges that could present themselves in real situations – they may look at your ability to solve problems, make decisions, delegate etc.

Tests can also be used find out how good you would be at doing some of the more **specific tasks** required to be successful in the opportunity you are applying for. This could be your keyboarding accuracy and speed, proofreading capability, special computer skills and so on.

Personality tests

These are not strictly tests as there are no right or wrong answers – because of this, they are sometimes known as personality questionnaires.

They are designed to find out about your personal characteristics that may or may not make you suitable for a particular opportunity. Although mainly used by large, public sector organisations, personality tests can form part of any job or course application process.

The questions explore the way you might react to, or deal with, different situations. The results of a personality test can indicate your preferred working or learning style, the way you might relate to other people, your ability to deal with your own emotions and the emotions of other people, what motivates you, how determined you are, your ability to lead or work in a team and how you could fit into the role or the culture of the organisation.

You can't practise personality tests – just give honest answers and don't spend too long thinking about each question. Also, don't try to guess what the selectors are looking for – you'll only be caught out. As the questions often involve using scales (e.g. from 1 to 6), make sure you know which end of the scale represents what!

Tips to help you tackle tests

Although there are lots of different tests, here's some general advice:

- if you know you have to do a test as part of the application process, try to find out what this will be and, if possible, do some practice tests

- if you have a special requirement, make sure that you tell someone at the organisation setting the test – they may be able to give you more time, provide the test in an alternative format or make allowances when looking at the results

- if it's up to you when you take the test, make sure that you set aside time when you aren't likely to be disturbed and when you're feeling in a positive frame of mind

- try to stay calm – there are usually some practice questions first to help you get going

- be aware that some tests include so many questions, few people would be expected to complete them in the time available – sometimes the questions get more complex as you go on

- read any instructions and each question very carefully

- if the test has to be done in a set time, work as quickly and as accurately as possible; don't spend too long pondering over one or two questions – you may be able to go back to them later, although this isn't always possible with online tests

- have a go at answering all the questions – at least a best guess gives you some chance of getting the question right!

N.B. Because it's usually impossible to check that you haven't had help with an online test taken at home, you may be asked to sit a similar test later in the selection process under controlled conditions.

Find out more about tests

Search the internet for websites that offer free practice tests, such as:

- www.psychometric-success.com

- www.shldirect.com

- www.morrisby.com.

There are lots of books on selection tests that include practice papers. Kogan Page is a major publisher of such books; titles include:

How to Pass Selection Tests – £8.99

Career, Aptitude and Selection Tests – £7.99

How to Master Psychometric Tests, How to Pass Verbal Reasoning Tests and *How to Pass Numeracy Tests* – £9.99 each

Ultimate Aptitude Tests and Ultimate Psychometric Tests – £9.99 each.

There are also books covering tests for entry to specific careers, such as the police, fire service and teaching.

Providing samples of your work

If you are applying for certain jobs, training programmes or courses, you may be asked to submit, along with your application form:

- one or more examples of work you have already produced in a job or on a course, **and/or**

- an exercise completed specifically for the opportunity.

Applying for jobs or training opportunities

You may be expected to provide samples of your work or to complete an exercise to demonstrate your potential to do a job or train for a career. So, if you're applying for training in journalism, you may have to submit an article you have had published; for a career in PR, you may be asked to write a press release; for a job in marketing, you could be asked to produce a marketing strategy. Other samples of your work may include drawings, designs, photographs etc.

A well-presented and creative portfolio of work is all-important if you want to apply for a job or training opportunity in a creative environment. If you have an online portfolio, you could give the link to this in your application.

Applying for courses

Some colleges and universities also ask you to supply examples of your work – perhaps from a current job role or course – or submit an essay or another piece of work. This may be a requirement for all applicants or only requested if you haven't studied for a while, or if you haven't got the usual entry requirements. If you're applying to university, the Entry Profiles on the UCAS website should indicate whether you will be asked to provide a portfolio of work, essay or other examples of your work.

If you are applying for a course in art and design, a portfolio of work is an important part of the application process. However, as mentioned above, you normally submit this after you have completed your application.

Other things to consider

- Find out whether you are expected to return your work samples or exercise by email or through the post. If the work is valuable or bulky, find out which postal service would be best.

- If you have to send work in the post, if at all possible, keep a copy.

- Depending on the opportunity, you could try contacting the organisation to ask whether it would be helpful to send a sample of your work along with your application. This can show initiative and may just get you noticed over the other applicants!

- If invited to an interview, it may be worth taking along any relevant samples of your work, if not asked for them earlier in the process.

Chapter eleven

After you've applied

This chapter:

- gives you tips on organising and following up your applications
- provides you with advice on what to do if you feel you're not getting anywhere
- tells you where you can get further information, advice and guidance.

Keeping track

If you apply for more than a couple of opportunities at a time, it's easy to get into a muddle – there's a danger that you'll lose important documents or, even worse, miss key deadlines! To avoid this, gather together everything associated with each opportunity you've applied for. This might include:

- the original advert, job or course description, person specification, organisation or course brochure, or anything else you may have been sent or found through research
- copies of your application form or CV, covering letter or email; any other correspondence.

You will need to refer to these documents if you get through to the next stage of the application process. Remember to organise both your electronic and paper-based information. So, if you've got emails or other documents on your computer, set up suitable folders where you can save these and make sure everything is clearly labelled.

Another way to keep organised is to produce a planner or log to summarise all the key information about each opportunity you have applied for. Use the example on page 121 as a starting point. You can adapt this to suit your needs and you could expand it to include interview dates etc.

Following up your applications

It may seem obvious, but you will need to routinely check your answerphone, mobile messages and email account in case you have had responses to your applications. If you apply for an opportunity online, you can sometimes track the progress of your application, so take advantage of this facility if it is available to you.

It can be frustrating having to wait to hear the outcome of an application. Due to systems within the organisation or the sheer volume of people applying, it can take a long time for selectors to go through all the forms or CVs. Course selection processes may take even longer than those for jobs.

If you have applied for an opportunity and you haven't heard anything a couple of weeks after the closing date, there's no harm ringing or emailing to find out if there has been any progress with your application – although avoid pestering them! It could be that there's been a delay of some sort or your application hasn't arrived.

Application planner

Vacancy/course title			
When opportunity advertised			
Where opportunity advertised			
Organisation			
Contact name/ job title			
Location			
Telephone			
Email			
Website			
Date details requested and how			
Date details received			
Closing date for applications			
Date application sent			
Application method (e.g. CV, form)			
Date should hear back			
Outcome and date			
Comments			

Sometimes you will be told that if you haven't heard from an organisation by a certain date, your application hasn't been successful. Similarly, you may be given the date/s that interviews will be held. If you're getting close to any of these dates, you could ring or email to check that your application has been received.

Unfortunately, some organisations leave you hanging. Despite it taking a lot of time and trouble for you to apply, they don't make the effort to let you know that you haven't been successful!

If you have sent in a CV on spec to a possible employer, a quick phone call or email may help to bring your information to the attention of someone within the organisation. You can also ask whether they are likely to have any vacancies in the future and request that they keep your CV on file in case a suitable vacancy arises.

Getting nowhere?

Don't despair! You can't expect to be called for an interview or get an offer every time you apply for an opportunity. Although it depends on how popular the opportunity is, usually only a small proportion of applicants get through to the next stage – and, in the case of most job vacancies, only one will be successful!

However, if it gets to the stage that you've applied for numerous opportunities and you still haven't had any interviews or offers, this is the time to step back and think why this might be. Why not email or phone to find out why you weren't selected for an opportunity? You may or may not receive honest feedback, but the selectors could give you some really useful tips for the future.

It could be that:

- there are just far too many people chasing the same opportunities as you

- you are applying for things that don't suit your skills, aptitudes, experiences and aspirations

- you still need to work on presenting yourself effectively in your CV and applications.

When there are few opportunities and lots of applicants, it can feel like the odds are against you. You may be tempted to start applying for anything and everything in order to increase your chances. However, selectors can usually spot applicants who are just going for any opportunity – they can't match their abilities to the entry requirements, they find it hard to show any real interest in the position, and they often end up sending standard CVs and applications just to save themselves time. Applicants who do this, therefore, also receive a lot of rejections!

To save yourself a great deal of time and disappointment, stay focused on those opportunities that best suit you. If you're enthusiastic and positive about an opportunity, this should come through in your application.

Be prepared, however, to think creatively about how to reach your goal. Is there anything you can do to improve your suitability? You could consider:

- trying to get some relevant work experience
- taking a course that will help you develop the skills you need or show your commitment
- looking further afield for opportunities
- applying for related opportunities that you could move on from once you have 'your foot in the door'.

If there's a chance that you're just not presenting yourself as effectively as you could be on paper, it's worth asking for help – sources of advice are listed at the end of this chapter.

Being discriminated against?

Despite laws protecting you from discrimination and efforts being made to monitor equal opportunities (see Chapter eight), if you feel that you have been discriminated against, for instance because of your age, race or gender, do seek advice. Talk the issue over with someone you trust, such as a tutor or personal/careers adviser. The organisations listed below should also be able to help.

Equality and Human Rights Commission – helpline for people living in England: 0845 604 6610; helpline for those in Wales: 0845 604 8810. You can also get information and advice by textphone, post, fax or email. For useful information and contact details, see: www.equalityhumanrights.com.

Acas (Advisory, Conciliation and Arbitration Service) – helpline: 08457 47 47 47. www.acas.org.uk.

For the address of your local **Citizens Advice Bureau**, look in the telephone directory or search through: www.citizensadvice.org.uk.

Information on your rights is also available on: www.adviceguide.org.uk.

General sources of information and advice

Your personal/careers adviser at your local Connexions/careers service can provide you with information, advice and guidance on applying for jobs, training and courses.

If you are aged 13-19, and live in England, you can contact **Connexions Direct** – tel: 080 800 13 2 19 or textphone: 08000 968 336. Useful information, including a facility to search for your local Connexions centre, can be found on: www.connexions-direct.com.

In England, information and advice for those aged 19+ may be available from advisers at your local **Next Step**. There's also lots of information on applying for jobs etc on: www.direct.gov.uk/nextstep.

If you live in Wales, information, advice and guidance is available from the all-age service, **Careers Wales**. Useful information and details of local offices are on: www.careerswales.com.

If you are unemployed and aged 19+, advisers at your local **Jobcentre Plus** will give you support in applying for jobs, training and courses. If you are younger than this, you can ask for similar help at your local Connexions/careers service.

Don't forget that there are lots of other people who will be happy to help you with your CV and applications – these may include, if you are at school or college, your teachers, tutor, careers teacher/coordinator, as well as your parent/s or carer/s, other members of your family and family friends.

Finally...

If you follow all the advice you've been given, keep trying and review your progress from time to time, you'll be much more likely to be invited to an interview or offered an opportunity. Most importantly, remember to stay positive!

For information on going for an interview, see the sister book to this one – *Excel at Interviews*.

Index

More titles in the Student Helpbook Series ...

helping students of all ages make the right choices about their careers and education.

Excel at Interviews – Tactics for job and college applicants

This highly successful book includes clear, impartial advice on everything students need to know to be prepared for their first interview.

6th edition £11.99   ISBN: 978 -904979-22-7

Decisions at 15/6+ – A guide to all your options

A comprehensive guide to help students choose their post-16 options. Includes information on different types of qualifications, training opportunities, where to study and applying.

12th edition £12.99   ISBN: 978-1-904979-45-6

Which A levels? – The guide to choosing A levels, Advanced Diplomas and other post-16 qualifications

The highly popular, student-friendly guide. Features over 50 AS/A level subjects and the range of Advanced Diplomas. Includes career options after A levels/Advanced Diplomas and as a graduate.

7th edition £14.99   ISBN: 978-1-904979-41-8

Jobs and Careers after A levels and equivalent advanced qualifications

Opportunities for students leaving school or college at 18, including advice on job-hunting, applications and interviews. Includes 40 engaging career profiles of young people working in a diverse range of occupations.

9th edition £11.99   ISBN: 978-1-904979-21-0

Careers with a Science Degree – Over 100 job ideas to inspire you

An excellent read for anyone considering science at degree level.

5th edition £12.99   ISBN: 978-1-904979-39-5

Careers with an Arts or Humanities Degree – Over 100 job ideas to inspire you.

An invaluable resource for anyone who wants to find out where an arts or humanities degree could lead.

5th edition £12.99   ISBN: 978-1-904979-40-1

Visit us online to view our full range of resources at:
www.lifetime-publishing.co.uk